To Jackie with best wishes and thanks

The Best of Times

Memoirs of a Countryman

George Briscoe

BY GEORGE BRISCOE

© George Briscoe 2005

Published by Bellinter Bridge Publications.
Tel: 046 9021474
E mail address: jgbriscoe@eircom.net

Printed in Ireland by Colour Books Ltd.
Typeset by Artwerk Ltd.

The dusk is down on the river meadows,
The moon is rising above the fir,
The lane is crowded with creeping shadows,
The gorse is but a distant blur.
The last of the light is almost gone,
But hark! They are running,
They are running on!

Will Ogilvie

For Jean

Acknowledgements

The idea of writing an account of my life was put to me over fifteen years ago by my great, late friend, Jim McAleese. My late, first wife, dear Louise, heartily endorsed the notion. I started to write and got about five chapters put together, but then, in spite of prodding from Jim and Louise, I lost the urge and got no further. This situation continued until after the death of Louise and Jim.

Not long after I married my lovely Jean, she put pressure upon me to continue with the project. At that stage I had almost forgotten about it. One day my very good friend, Paddy FitzGerald, was down in the house when Jean raised the subject. Paddy asked to have a look at what I had done. I produced a black-covered notebook that contained my *oeuvre*. Paddy took it away with him and put it up on his computer. He requested more, which I later wrote and gave to him. After that the two of us had several interviews that Paddy recorded and later transcribed. Later on he knocked it into the shape it is in now. If it had not been for Paddy I doubt if this book would have been produced. I am grateful to him for all his work.

I wish to thank Michael FitzGerald for having reproduced all the photographs, many of which are old and of poor quality, including some of which were as newspaper and magazine cuttings, and also for the reproduction of the painting and prints contained herein. Finally, I thank the eminent artist, John Ryan for permission to reproduce his painting of the spiral staircase at Bellinter House.

George Briscoe,
Craystown House, Bective,
Navan, Co. Meath,
November 2005.

List of Contents

1. Birth and Home

FROM early 1919 until July 1921, Ireland was convulsed by the Anglo Irish War, which raged throughout the greater part of the country. The war signified an attempt by the Irish to gain independence from the British and to secede from the United Kingdom of Great Britain and Ireland. On the Irish side, the war was characterised by guerrilla tactics and by attacks on police barracks and on British military personnel. British reaction featured the burning of towns, terrorism and executions. Under pressure from public opinion in the United States of America and in Britain, the British government sought a cease-fire. On 11 July 1921 a truce was agreed when it was arranged that representatives of Sinn Féin should negotiate with the British in London.

I entered the world shortly after the truce had been called, and in a relatively peaceful lacuna in Irish history. The date was 29 July 1921; the place was a nursing home in Dublin. After a few days in Dublin I was taken to my parents' home at Bellinter. At that time Bellinter House was not in use by the family. We lived for some years in a house in the yard.

Bellinter House is situated overlooking the River Boyne, between Navan and Trim in County Meath. During the Anglo-Irish war the Irish Republican Army destroyed many large country houses. Thankfully, Bellinter survived unharmed.

Following on from the Anglo-Irish war, more trouble soon arrived. In October 1921 the treaty between the Irish and the British was signed to the satisfaction of the British but to the division of the Irish. There was a majority on the Irish side who accepted the limited independence that gave Ireland the authority to run its own affairs as a 26 county state. However, there was a minority who wanted the creation of a republic and complete independence from

Britain. Shortly after the treaty had been passed by a majority in the Irish parliament in early January of 1922, the Irish began fighting among themselves. A civil war, which lasted until May 1923, broke out. The outcome saw the defeat of the republicans by the Army of the Free State. Peace was restored.

Bellinter was designed by the famous eighteenth century English architect, Richard Casells around 1750 and built over several years shortly afterwards. It is a great stone house with two comparatively large wings. The wings are joined to the main block by an orangery on the east side and by a passage way and steps on the west side which adjoin the large kitchen and servants' quarters.

There are four very big corner rooms on the first floor in the main block. These were beautiful rooms with pitch pine panelling. Along with two other, smaller rooms, they were used as bedrooms. The upper storey of the main house was set aside for children's accommodation. There were bedrooms, a nursery, a schoolroom and the governess's quarters. Servants were accommodated in the west wing, which was a house in itself. On the ground floor there was a drawing groom, a dining room, a morning room, a breakfast room and a few other rooms.

It was always a matter of some amazement to me to know how hot meals were produced from the wing when all the food had to be carried from the kitchen down to the basement and across to the east side of the house and up more stairs to the dining room. I believe it was for just this situation that large households possessed big covers, which were put over the roasts to help them keep warm on their journey. Nowadays such covers are rarely seen. The very large range cooker practically stretched the length of one wall in the kitchen. The amount of coal consumed must have been enormous. My father told me that he remembered the coal carts going to and from the station at Navan drawing home the supply for winter. In my time Bellinter was as cold as hell in cold weather. My wife and I used to almost have to barricade ourselves into the library with a roaring fire. Whenever we left the room a blast of cold air almost took our breath away. We were living in an interim period since central heating was in its infancy. In my grandfather's time every fire in the house upstairs and downstairs was lit each morning during the winter months.

Entrance to the house is by a wide flight of stone steps that leads into a great hall, which has some very fine plasterwork and ceiling. There is a magnificent fireplace into which one could place very large pieces of timber, which would keep burning for a long time and help to put some heat into the main block of the house. Opening off the hall are two very fine drawing rooms, breakfast room, library, dining room and entrance to the inner hall and very impressive stairs to the first floor and also an entrance hall to the back stairs. These are circular stairs coming from the basement to the top storey. They are unique in this country and it is quite an extraordinary feat of architecture that the outer part of the circular stair is supported for four storeys by the bottom outside step.

The two large drawing rooms were most elegant. One had a beautiful Italian ceiling. Both had silk paper on the walls, which had been there since the house was built. It was quite magnificent. The capacity of these rooms could be judged by the fact that we had many hunt balls for the Tara Harriers and the Meath Hunt and had 400 guests who all enjoyed a sit-down supper. It was a wonderful house for those functions and the parties went on until 7 or 8 o'clock in the morning. My trouble, if one can call it such, was that one of the bars was set up in my bedroom! The smell of drink for a while would certainly have put the faint hearted off the booze forever; however, I survived.

There were some very fine mantelpieces. There was a Bossi, an Adams and a really beautiful one in the small drawing room, which had come from Dean Swift. His

connection with Bellinter is interesting. On the death of the
dean many of his personal possessions went to his great
friend, Ford of Woodparc, Dunboyne. My grandfather, after
inheriting Bellinter, owned Woodparc and from there he
brought some of the dean's original possessions amongst
which were portraits of Stella, Vanessa and of the dean.
Jarvis, a well-known portrait painter of the time, painted all
of them. They are known as the Woodparc Collection.

For some years before I was born, my father rented out
Bellinter demesne to Leslie Brabazon who was a horse
trainer. At that time Bellinter House was boarded up and
remained unoccupied. During those years my father lived in
Tralee but, upon his marriage, he returned with my mother
to Bellinter. When I was born in 1921 my parents had been
living in quite a nice house in the yard and we continued to
do so up to about 1930.

Until about 1930 at Bellinter there was no running water
and lighting was by gas lamps. Open fires that were fuelled by
coal and wood provided heating. Before 1930 water for the
house was drawn from wells. There was a well on the east
side of the house and another on the west side. In the yard
there was another well from which water was drawn up by a
hand-operated pump. Not having water in the house meant
that we did not have water closets. At a distance of about
fifty yards from the entrance to the house, in the woods,
there was an enclosed and roofed, five-seat dry lavatory. I
remember sitting on it as a child. My grandfather had his
initials carved on one of the seats and dare anybody be sitting
on that when he came in! Oh, I often sat with someone else.
We were very communal. That was the way. Writing about
this, I am reminded of the old rhyme:

> *In days of old when men were bold*
> *And paper hadn't been invented*
> *They wiped their arse with a piece of grass*
> *And walked away contented.*

When my father inherited a bit of money in about 1930 from his uncle, FitzHenry Smith of Duleek, he carried out quite a few improvements to the place and, having done so, we moved into the big house. Apart from money, my father also inherited at the same time, sporting rights in Cos. Donegal and Tyrone. Included in these rights are shooting rights over a large amount of land and fishing rights on the Derg River. I retain those rights to the present.

Grouse shooting up there was very good and the Derg River is very good for salmon and trout. During the Second World War when U.S. troops were based up around Derry, they shot the hell out of the place and ruined it. My father got fed up and after that he didn't bother to shoot there anymore.

Getting back to improvements, my father had a large generator installed in a room of its own in the east wing and had the house wired up. Beside the generator, in another room, there were from fifty to sixty large batteries that had open tops. During the summer, depending upon what was used, the batteries would keep us going for a month or six weeks. In the winter the batteries stored enough electricity to last a fortnight or three weeks, depending upon the drain. In order to recharge the batteries we usually ran the generator for a day. We had a big electric board that we switched in for recharging. Electricity that was generated was at 110 volts that we mostly used for lighting but, in the winter, we also used some heaters. Light that was provided by the generator was as good as that later given by the Electricity Supply Board (E.S.B.).

The generator was a very large diesel *Petar* engine that was very noisy and, sometimes, very difficult to start. In order to start the engine I had to light a cartridge, like a shotgun cartridge, and then to screw it down quickly into a tube at the top of the engine and then start to crank the engine. The engine was turned until it fired and then off it went. It was a very, very heavy engine to crank. I usually had to get a man or two on the belt that ran between the engine proper and the generator. It was a great help to have someone pulling the belt while I was cranking the engine. Sometimes it was very difficult. If it fired straight away, well and good; however, if it didn't fire straight away, it was exhausting work cranking and cranking. Having said that, it was a great engine. We had it up to the late 1940s when rural electrification was introduced and when we changed over to the E.S.B.

I sold the whole outfit for practically nothing. Selling it really went to my heart because it had been a most efficient system, but, I suppose, it couldn't have lasted forever. In a way I was pleased that my cranking days were over. I used to get hell from both my mother and from my wife, Louise. They both said that I'd kill myself twisting that yoke. As I have said, it was alright when it used to start on the first go but oftentimes it didn't and I'd be there twisting and cranking with the sweat rolling off me and my arm aching.

During improvements, my father had a colossal tank put up in the attics, had the place plumbed and had a water pump installed on the bank of the River Boyne to pump water up to the tank. The pump was another eccentric piece of equipment. It had to be started by heating the underside of it with a blowlamp. That also took a bit of cranking. When the pump got going, it would take a day or longer to fill the tank. An overflow pipe led off from the tank into the eaves. When we saw water coming out of this, we turned the pump off, as we knew that the tank was full. A full tank used to last for about two weeks or so. The days of the dry lavatory in the woods were over!

My grandfather, Gussie Briscoe, had a billiards table put in the hall. We used to have many games of billiards and slosh. Snooker was not popular in those days and we rarely played it. It wasn't as it is today, very popular. Billiards was the most popular game that we played. We used to have hours of great fun.

In the yard there was a long row of buildings that housed a big laundry in which there was a huge clothes dryer. There was also a slaughterhouse where the animals to be slaughtered were kept in cages. As well as that there was a carpentry shop. On the other side there was a coach house and stables for horses.

At a distance of about a half a mile from the house and down near the garden there was an icehouse. This was built of limestone and was set down at its site and covered with a pile of earth. I remember it well; it was igloo-shaped. It was very dark inside, but I suppose that the servants, when they were stocking it with ice from frozen ponds in the wintertime, used oil lamps for illumination.

The garden, to which I have adverted, was a good distance from the house. Going to it from the house was by way of a beautiful walk through a lovely wood of oak, beech and other species. In the garden there was a magnificent, long, brick-faced wall that was heated by water pipes passing through it. It must have been about twenty feet high, faced towards the south and, against it fruit trees were grown in *espalier* fashion. A wood-burning boiler provided the hot water. Also in the garden there was an orangery. Lady Tara is reputed to have been the first person to have grown oranges in Ireland.

Taking up about two acres, the garden was in the centre of a beautiful wood and, as is usually the case, it was not walled but rather it was enclosed by a beautiful beech hedge. It was quite magnificent.

Up to the time that the Wyndham Act was passed in 1903, the Bellinter Estate consisted of between 10,000 and 15,000 acres that were scattered in small farms, mostly in County Meath but in other counties also. Kilmessan village was on the estate. Both the Catholic church and the Church of Ireland church were built on Bellinter ground in Kilmessan. Land for both graveyards was given either by

John Preston or by my grandfather, Gussie, to the Churches. Gussie presented the bell to the Catholic church. It was a very good bell, a very loud one. It also served as a weather forecaster for Gussie because, with the prevailing wind coming from the southwest, Gussie knew that if he could hear the bell clearly at Bellinter that rain was on the way.

2. Family

THE family of Briscoe comes of ancient stock, originally English, but is long settled in Ireland. John Briscoe, A.D.C. to General Coote, is said to have been an officer in Queen Elizabeth the first's army against O'Neill, Earl of Tyrone. He married Eleanor Kearney of Scraghe, near Tullamore, Co. Offaly. In 1588 he built the castle of Scraghe, adjacent to the Kearney family house. John Briscoe is said to have been of the family of Crofton Hall, Cumberland. Of interest is the presence of a small town that is situated about two miles to the southeast of Carlisle in Cumberland and which bears the name, Brisco.

Within a couple of centuries of the construction of the castle at Scraghe, people of the name Briscoe held lands in the counties, Dublin, Kilkenny, Mayo Offaly, Tipperary and Westmeath.

MacLysaght, in his book, *The Surnames of Ireland*, states that the name, Briscoe, is an English toponymic and that it has been in Ireland since the sixteenth century but is not closely identified with any county.

My immediate family came from Kilkenny. They owned a great deal of land there and the family seat was Tinvane near Carrick-on-Suir, which town was in our possession up to my father's time. My great grandfather, Francis, was a clergyman who, in the middle of the nineteenth century, was rector of Kilmessan. My grandfather, Gussie, was a very great friend of John Joseph Preston of Bellinter, who was a son of Lord Tara, but who declined to accept the title. He was a fine sportsman and owned some really top racehorses, the most famous being *Brunette*. She was one of the great steeplechase mares of all time.

My great grandfather's brother, Henry Briscoe, who was born in 1809, was a very famous master and huntsman of the

Kilkenny Hounds in his early years. After his marriage to Deborah Shaw he established a pack of hounds of his own which he called the Tinvane Hounds. Having hunted this pack for eight seasons, he sold it to the Marquis of Waterford for the latter to form the Curraghmore Hounds. Henry continued to hunt. In 1870 he was invited to become master of the Kilkenny Hounds but had to resign in 1876 because of ill health. On his retirement he received a testimonial in the shape of a well-filled purse and a resolution of thanks for the fine sport he had afforded, as well for the state in which he had left the pack, which as the resolution, proposed by Sir James Langrishe, expressed it, was in a state of 'unsurpassed efficiency.' Henry was known by many as the *John Peel of Ireland*.

Lord Tara of Bellinter founded the Tara Harriers as the Bellinter Harriers in the 1750s. John Preston, son of Lord Tara, was also a very keen hunting man and became the second master of the Bellinter Harriers. He had married but had no family and on his death he left Bellinter and his estate of a great deal of land to Gussie Briscoe. The will was contested but Gussie Briscoe won the case. He ran the estate for John Preston and took over on his death in 1890. My grandfather became the third master and it was he who renamed the pack, the Tara Harriers. Gussie, my grandfather, was succeeded in the mastership of the Tara Harriers by his son-in-law, E.W. Hope-Johnston of Tribley, Kilmessan. The fifth master was W. Dove of Kilcarne.

My father once told me an interesting story about Lord Tara. Like all major landlords, he had an agent. Sometime in the early 1800s his agent approached him about accommodation. The agent said to Lord Tara that there was no unoccupied, suitable house on the estate in which he could live. Lord Tara chose a site for him in the townland of Balsoon, about one and half miles to the southwest of Bellinter House. Lord Tara told his agent that, as he, Lord Tara, was going off to Australia for a considerable time that the house should be finished upon his return. Anyway, off he went to Australia, what doing, I don't know. On his return after a year or more, he was astonished to see that his agent had a large, country mansion built for himself. That is how Balsoon House came into existence.

In 1881 Gussie, an only child, married Amy Smith from Duleek whose family owned many large properties in Meath, including Bessborough, Brierley, Duleek House, Annesbrook and Dunmoe, thus uniting two large land-owning families in the county.

This is probably an appropriate time to tell a story of one of the many escapades of my grandfather, Gussie Briscoe. After a very hilarious dinner party in which no doubt most had imbibed far too much, Gussie was wagered that he would not ride a horse up the circular stairs! He did it but going up was one thing, coming down was almost impossible. I often wondered in my young days why there was a large beam across the very top. This was the proof that it happened as there was no way they could get the horse down until the beam was put in and from which he was winched down in the centre of the staircase. How long the horse had been detained in the attics I do not know.

Gussie was a very well known and popular figure in Meath. He was High Sheriff for many years. He took over running the estate at a very difficult time. The tenants to a large extent were both poor and rebellious. He was, however, a very humane man and would on no account ever evict a tenant. Although this eventually almost ruined him financially, he never regretted it and in fact, the last thing he said to my father when dying was "never evict a tenant". Gale days were held twice a year when the tenants came to pay their rent and this entailed barrels of beer and dancing. The predominant procedure was for the tenant to string a great tale of woe and state an inability to pay, whereupon Gussie would say "ah, pay me when you can," which usually meant never.

However, in spite of all this, he managed to live a very full and exciting life.

Gussie Briscoe had an ocean-going yacht, which he kept at Drogheda. My father told me several stories concerning this. He used to sail up around Scotland, through the Caledonian Canal and sometimes out into the North Sea. One incident, of which he should not have been too proud, was when he threw a stick of dynamite into a very well known salmon pool somewhere in Scotland. The stunned fish came to the surface and he picked out a nice one. This did not kill the fish and soon the rest recovered and swam away unhurt.

One can imagine what wonderful times they must have enjoyed in those trips. He used to rent a house near Clifden in Connemara for part of the summer. He arranged the dispatch by train of all the paraphernalia such as cows for milk, dogs, etc. and he would sail the yacht around southern Ireland and up to Clifden. I understand they had many exciting and very rough passages on this voyage. The yacht was called *Amy* after his wife. The old bell from the boat was in the hall in Bellinter up to the time of the sale of Bellinter and got lost or mislaid when we moved from there to Bective.

He took over Bellinter Harriers, the name of which he changed to Tara Harriers, in honouring a wish in John Preston's will that this should be so. He had many years of good sport with the harriers.

John Watson, who lived at Bective House, was a famous master of the Meath Hunt at the beginning of the twentieth century. He was a very overbearing and autocratic man and most people were very much in awe of him. There were many large estates in Meath at that time and Watson did not "warn", as we do now, but told the owners he was coming and frowned very much on any large owner making objections. My grandfather, Gussie, had a pet fox and one day that the hounds were coming to hunt in Bellinter he could not find his pet fox. He asked John not to draw the garden wood, as that was where his fox usually lived. John, on arrival, went straight to the garden wood and killed the pet fox at the front door of Bellinter. Gussie of course was furious and could not agree to John Watson's autocratic and bullying tactics. Gussie planned to get his revenge.

Gussie planned to lay a drag hunt and had been trying for a long time but could not get anything that John's hounds would hunt. A substance called 'Renardine' came on the market. Gussie tried it on his own hounds and they hunted it. Thereupon he got several men and ran a drag for about 20 miles. John's hounds hunted perfectly and he was going around saying that was one of the best hunts he had ever had. Gussie had a large party in Bellinter at the end of the season and all having wined and dined well he got up and said "John that was marvellous hunt you had but I just want to tell you it was a drag." Rumour had it that Watson was fit to shoot him.

Another story that I think is worth recording concerns Gussie, a man called Harry Dyas, who was well-known because his horse, *Manifesto*, had won the Aintree Grand National and a couple of others. They went off one day shooting snipe. Unfortunately, the heavens opened so they retired to the nearest pub. They spent the rest of the day there and were not in great shape when they returned to Bellinter that evening for dinner. "Well Harry, did you have a good day's shooting?" asked Amy. "Yes Amy, we had a marvellous day snoop shiting."

In the horseracing world, Gussie had two significant wins in his time. In 1894 he won the Galway Plate with a chestnut horse called *Star One*. This was trained by G.L. Walker and ridden by E. Reilly. The horse started at 8/1 and the prize money was 125 pounds. A short time later, in 1896 he won the Irish Grand National at Fairyhouse with his horse, *Royston-crow*. Again, the trainer was G.L. Walker. The jockey was L. Parsons. *Royston-crow* had a starting price of 6/1 and won 245 pounds for Gussie.

In the late nineteen nineties Gussie was the cause of a fair bit of controversy in the country. Members of the British Israel Association of London approached Gussie and told him that they believed that the Ark of the Covenant was buried on the historic Hill of Tara, part of which he owned at the time. They told him that he had a duty to permit them to excavate in the part of the hill that he owned, in order to search for the Ark. Unwisely, Gussie gave his permission. Excavation began in the summer of 1899 and continued sporadically until the summer of 1902. A lot of pressure had been brought to bear in order to have the exploratory work stopped. Gussie enjoyed the notoriety for a while but afterwards tired of the whole affair. He sold the land in 1903 under the terms of the Wyndham Act.

Gussie and Amy had two sons and four daughters. Eileen Dora, born 1882, married Roguey Hope-Johnston who owned a very large house and estate called Raehills in Dumfrieshire, Scotland. They lived for some time at Tribley, Bective, and in fact, Roguey was master of the Tara Harriers for a couple of years while residing there. Eileen, like all the Briscoe girls of that generation, was a superb horsewoman. Tragically, she died in 1909 aged 27 when giving birth to their son, Percy. Roguey, some time later married May Domvile and they lived for some years in Clonhugh on Lough Owell where he was master of the Westmeath Hunt.

John Joseph was born in 1883. He never married and was not very robust and died in 1913.

Amy Maura, born in 1884, died at the age of 10 of appendicitis from having eaten raisins that had been put out for the pheasants.

Cecil Henry, my father, was born in 1886. He was very keen on engineering and after being at school at Uppingham and Portora he went as an apprentice to work in a company owned by one of Gussie's friends, Sir Charles Marham, in Cheshire. All was going well for him until his brother died and he had to come home to take over the running of Bellinter as his mother was not able to cope with it.

In 1909 my father became sixth master of the Tara Harriers and served in that capacity until 1914. At the time of the outbreak of the Great War, a good many young Irishmen volunteered to serve in the British Army. However, my father was not fit to join up because of a shooting accident a few years earlier when he was over at Roguey's place in Scotland. On that occasion he was at a pheasant shoot when something went wrong with his gun. Roguey had a pair of brand new Purdeys and he lent one of them to my father. The group had shot just less than 300 hundred pheasant when they decided to beat into another wood to try to get the total to the 300 mark. A pheasant flew up and my father shot it. Upon putting down the gun, an outside pocket of his coat caught the trigger guard and the gun fell onto the ground in front of him, went off and blew the big toe off one of his feet and badly damaged the rest of the foot. He was always very lame after that. Even so, he was lucky that it had not been worse.

During the war he worked with remount horses in Belfast, breaking them in for the soldiers. That was his contribution to the war effort. When breaking horses in Belfast an animal threw him off and he landed heavily on the bottom of his back onto a stone water trough. He hurt his back severely and was never able to ride again. After that he was fairly crippled.

My father struggled through some very difficult times including the economic war with Britain, but managed to keep his head above water. In 1919 he married my mother, Phyllis Stawell Heard. She was a daughter of George Bennet Heard whose family owned a lovely, old place near Kinsale, called Coolmain Castle.

My elder sister, Constance, who was born in 1919, first married Peter Moor, a British army man. She has a son, Michael, by this marriage. Michael carries on a successful accountancy practice in Dublin. Her second husband, Major

Nick Morrogh-Ryan, was also in the British army. On his retirement, they managed Castle Leslie for Anita King for some years. Later they managed Streamstown House in Co. Westmeath for the Italian owners. They enjoyed good hunting when there. They have a daughter, Nicola, who is married to John Maxwell. Nick Morrogh-Ryan's family had Dunboyne Castle for many years and Nick's grandfather was a well-known master of the Ward Union Stag Hounds.

Stella, my younger sister, was born in 1926. She married Lancelot Smith of Donabate in 1948. He was a farmer and spent his winters for many years as master and huntsman of several packs. He started with the Fingal Harriers and graduated from there to the East Galway Hounds, to the Blazers, to the Island in Wexford, and finally, to the Meath Hunt.

They have a son, Henry, and a daughter, Hilary. Hilary married and has a son and lives in Australia. Henry has a family and is now carrying on the Briscoe association with the Tara Harriers, being joint master and huntsman.

Stella was a very good horsewoman and apart from whipping in for a number of the packs with which Lance was involved, she won a number of point-to-point races and show jumping events.

Another sister of my father, Gladys, was born in 1888. She was a well-known horsewoman and a great judge of a horse. She was first married to Eyre Massy and had a son, Luke and a daughter, Beatrice. Luke was a joint master of the Tara Harriers with me from 1942 to 1955. He was a well-known character and up to many pranks and devilment. Gladys later married Cecil Brabazon from the well-known racing family in Westmeath from which marriage she also had a son, Aubrey, and a daughter, Lelia. Aubrey became one of the great steeplechase riders of Ireland. Lelia was an excellent rider in her younger days and won many shows. She is one of my favourite cousins.

Lelia married Paddy Harboard after the Second World War and went to live on the Curragh in Co. Kildare where Paddy set up the Curragh Bloodstock Agency, which he ran successfully for many years. Paddy had gone to fight in the war and was captured early on in the action so that he was a prisoner for most of the duration of the campaign. He had a very tough time of it. He used to tell us things that one would hardly believe. One day he told me that when he was in the prison camp that the food was so scarce and so bad that he used to catch rats, skin them and cook them in order to keep going. When he was freed and returned home when the war had ended, his blood had been affected by his diet.

On the Curragh there are lots of sheep that roam freely around to graze and can sometimes cause dreadful nuisance. Sheep broke into Lelia's and Paddy's garden early one morning. They both went out in their dressing gowns to get them out when a wasp stung Paddy on the lip. Within a few minutes he started to stagger around the place. Lelia said, "What's wrong, what's wrong?" "Oh, I feel awful," said Paddy. Lelia managed to get him into the house and into bed. She called for the doctor, who was there within the hour. However, poor Paddy was dead before he got there.

This brings us to the last of that generation, Muriel Georgina, called Babs. She was the only one of the sisters with whom I hunted and I always held her in awe. She was quite fearless and was such a superb horsewoman that one really felt one had achieved something if able to stay with her.

She first married Hugh Malcolmson of the well-known family from Portlaw, Waterford. They were unique in that one time they issued leather tokens, which were accepted as legal currency. He was killed in the First World War. There were two daughters and a son of the marriage. George, their son, was known all over the country and was very close to me. In fact, he was more like a brother than a cousin. He was master of the Ward Union Stag Hounds for many years, was a fine shot and fisherman.

He owned some good racehorses, the best known being *Pontet*. She was bought by his mother in the sales for 10 pounds and was given to him. She won the Irish Grand National in 1937 ridden by Eric McKeever. She was next to run in the Conyngham Cup at Punchestown but unfortunately Eric McKeever was hurt and unable to ride. Our uncle, Cecil Brabazon, who trained her said to George "Why don't' you get up and ride her yourself?"

There was considerable work getting him fit and then the great day came. He rode a marvellous race and won. There were great celebrations and I well remember going to my first hunt ball in Naas that night. I had no proper evening clothes but I got rigged out with bits and pieces from various people. Uncle Cecil had lent me his trousers as he said he would not go. I was enjoying my first ball when he appeared and said that he had changed his mind and that he wanted his trousers back and handed me another pair. Unfortunately they were far too small and I was the object of great mirth when I appeared with the trousers almost up to my knees.

The elder daughter, Emm, was a most attractive girl. She hunted a lot with the Wards and was a very accomplished ballroom dancer.

The younger daughter, Eileen, who was always known as 'Dan', married Randal Lannigan-O'Keeffe, from Co. Clare and who was a prominent member of the staff of Jackson, Stops and McCabe, the well-known estate agents. Dan was a very good horsewoman and had a first class knowledge of horses. She judged in many shows both here and overseas. Her daughter, Susan, had been joint master of the Tara Harriers with me from 1977 until she retired in 1999.

3. School Days

OF THE first few years of my life I am naturally very hazy. However, I can remember the interest that I had shown and the excitement I felt whenever I used to see my father, who was a very accomplished sportsman, go off shooting or fishing. Of course, like any small child, there was the excitement of going to the beach for the day or going to the pantomime or to a party. I believe that I rode my first small pony when I was five years old but I did not become very keen on riding until I was about fourteen. My two sisters, Constance and Stella, one older than me and one younger, were accomplished horsewomen at a young age. It always seemed to me that girls took to the saddle much earlier than boys.

I was launched into my first real experience of life at the age of seven and a half years by having been sent off to school at Deganway in North Wales. This I resented terribly and apart from going to school, I hated leaving my lovely home in Ireland. The practice of sending small children away to school was quite common at that time but I always considered that it was somewhat cruel sending children of that age so far away. I did have consolation in that my grandfather and grandmother on my mother's side lived beside the school and took me out on most Sundays. I also had two very good friends from Ireland there, the late Dick Musgrave, later Sir Richard, and his brother, Michael, who was tragically killed right at the end of the war.

Boats and trains were of course, exciting to young boys and we had many trips on these as we travelled back after each term and over again for the beginning of the next. The mail boats from Dun Laoghaire to Holyhead in those days were built more for speed than comfort and we experienced very many rough crossings. During one such rough passage I walked up on deck and got to the windward side of a fair lady at the wrong moment and received the contents of her stomach in the face.

Woodlands, Deganwy, was a good school no doubt. We learned I suppose as much as we had to learn to get us on to our next school. I was always very keen on games, but soccer and cricket took precedence there although rugby was what I really loved. We played a little there but not enough for my liking.

At Woodlands, one instance stands out in my mind and makes me marvel how much medical science has advanced since those days. I had not been feeling well for some days and had a nasty pain in my abdomen, which got worse and worse. The school doctor consistently pronounced that there was nothing wrong with me until I was in such pain that I got in touch with my grandfather. As soon as he saw me he insisted on a second opinion and while bringing me into Llandudno I suffered a burst appendix. I spent about a month between life and death with tubes hanging from me. No doubt I can thank my grandfather for my first escape from death.

I left Woodlands at the age of 13 and was booked into Portora Royal School, Enniskillen, Co Fermanagh. This appealed to me so much more than my last place. I still did not fancy school very much however, as I was then almost 14 and taking a very great interest in riding, shooting and fishing. There were 800 acres in the family demesne that had an abundance of game, a wonderful trout stream, and with salmon to be caught on the Boyne. I now also had my own pony, as did my two sisters, and we used to hack off many miles to meets of the Meath Foxhounds. We thought nothing of distances then and we had to hack, as we had no other transport. I remember after a long hunt out near the sea near Gormanstown hacking 22 miles home with my sister and getting home in the pitch dark. That was the procedure all the time during Christmas holidays from Portora.

I had a good and happy time at Portora. It was an excellent choice of school for me because it was out in the country amidst surroundings that I loved. I must admit, however, that the real reason I was sent there was because it was a great school and my father had been educated there.

Academically I never hit any highlights although I did reach sixth form and became second head of the school. My father had been crippled for many years and it had always been understood that on leaving school I would come back and run the estate and farm, so therefore, it seemed pointless studying for exams when I was not going to go on to university.

The games and sport were very good. Portora was a very fine rugby school and the last year I was there we got to the semi-final of the Ulster School's Senior Cup competition. We could play cricket or row in the summer. I opted for rowing which I loved. I never was much of a cricketer anyway.

Rowing is a tough, hard sport. One had to be very fit. We learned the sport in what were called *tubs*. These were quite wide boxes with two rowers and with the instructor in the stern. I do recall that on one occasion I caught such a crab that I upended the boat and we all sank, luckily, with no dire consequences. I might add that we rowed in a stretch of water that was called *The Narrows*, which joined Upper and Lower Lough Erne. There is a very strong current there and before we were allowed to row we had to be able to swim across the stretch and back again. I was a reasonably good swimmer but I found it very hard to do. However, it was a very safe precaution in order to avoid being drowned.

On another occasion when rowing for the second four against the first four, we were winning easily when the bow at the back of my rowing shorts got stuck in the roller seat. I couldn't move but able only to dip my oar in and out of the water. We still won the race. However, there were quite a few people on the landing pier, including women. Try as I could there was no way I could loosen my shorts. All the fly buttons had broken off and I was fully exposed! There was nothing I could do, so amongst great hilarity, we arrived at the pier and I had to be extricated!

It was here with my friend for all his too short life, Waring Willis, that I learned a considerable amount about hunting hounds. The Fermanagh Harriers were kennelled about three and a half miles from the school. Whenever we could manage to get out for a few hours in the afternoon, Waring and I ran out to the kennels as fast as possible, took out the hounds and hunted for as long as we could, leaving ourselves time to get back to school in time for classes. We did have pangs of conscience having left the hounds to be collected by the kennel man. However, fortunately there was never any damage done or a hound lost.

The headmaster when I first went to Portora was a Mr. Seale, who had been there for a great number of years. It was just like *Tom Brown's School Days*. When the doors were opened for lunch' there was a mad rush to grab a potato or whatever else was on the table, otherwise, one had no lunch'. Certainly, it was the survival of the fittest. If we missed breakfast twice in a week we got three of the best on the backside on Saturday. I don't believe this ever did any of us any harm. Mr Seale's successor, a Mr Stuart, abolished the cane but if we were late for breakfast the doors were closed and we got none. We found this a much worse punishment.

Mr Stuart modernised the school a great deal but because of the extra cost of better food, improved dormitories and so forth, he was not popular with the board of governors who were a very antiquated and conservative lot.

There was an incident concerning one of Portora's most famous past pupils, Oscar Wilde. The large hall had many plaques around the walls commemorating famous alumni. The plaque dedicated to the memory of Wilde had been removed because of his jailing for homosexual practices. Through the influence of Mr Stuart on the board of governors, the plaque was restored.

I left Portora in 1939 having made many good friends. My best friend at Portora was the late Bill Milligan who was in class with me. Bill's younger brother, Pat, is now my best, old friend from that school. Pat had a very interesting and adventurous life that included tin mining in Nigeria for many years.

The school was a good school and a happy one and I believe it gave me a very good start in life.

4. Lord Dunsany, Senator Quirke

DURING the Anglo-Irish war, Lord Dunsany, the author and patron of the Slane poet, Francis Ledwidge, had a gamekeeper called Twomey. Sportsmen were not allowed to have guns or cartridges at the time. My father had two or three guns, which he used to hide under the billiards table. He came home one day and to his consternation his guns were gone. Through the grapevine he heard that Twomey, who was one of the top men in the IRA at the time, had taken his guns.

There was a very good duck shoot on the Boyne below Bellinter and Lord Dunsany appeared one day and went down shooting duck. One evening shortly after that my father was dining with the officer in charge of the Auxiliaries and remarked that it was damned annoying that he could not have a gun while Dunsany could come down and shoot his duck. The officer said, "Oh, I'll have to see about that."

Shortly afterwards my father was in Dublin in the Stephen's Green Club when General Hammond, who was Lord Dunsany's agent, rushed in and seeing my father said "Cecil, something awful has happened, they have arrested Eddie and put him in Beggar's Bush jail for having a gun and ammunition, we will have to go and bail him out." My father was amused to realize that he was the person responsible for putting him in and was the first to be asked to go and bail him out.

When all the activities were over my father was in the Russell Arms Hotel in Navan one day when a man came in and said to him "Would you like to get your guns back, Mr. Briscoe?" He did not know who the man was but said, "I certainly would." Time went by and my father was in the hotel again when the same man came up and said, "Did you get your guns back alright?" "No" said my father. "Oh, I'll see about that." A few evenings later my father was going out to dinner and met Twomey on his bicycle with three guns tied along the crossbar and so ended that saga. I still shoot with one of them, a very nice Truloch & Harris.

After my father had got badly hurt in 1914, the Tara Harriers were in abeyance until 1935. Senator Bill Quirke bought Ringlestown House at that time and came down to Bellinter to see my father with the idea of having the hunt revived. He was a partner in Stokes & Quirke, an auction-eering firm in County Tipperary. He loved horses and hunting which he had been doing all his life in his native county. A senator, he was very well known and a very influential man with Eamonn DeValera. My father was delighted and with the help of quite a number of local sportsmen, doctors, lawyers etc, he purchased some hounds and got them going again. The old kennels at Bellinter were repaired and so they resumed hunting in Meath. Bill hunted them until 1942 and then with pressure of work he handed the horn over to me. In the meantime the Kill Harriers over in the Longwood-Ballivor end had gone defunct and the Taras were asked by a number of farmers in that end to come over and hunt their country. This was agreed and my first cousin, Luke Massey, who lived at Perth House, Enfield, took the horn to hunt that end.

Around this time, Lockes' Distillery in Kilbeggan came on the market and Bill Quirke got the sale of it for his firm. It became a very dragged out affair with foreigners involved and Bill trying madly to clinch a deal. He was hard to be found and people used to ring me to know if I had any idea where he was. This prompted two rather amusing little bits of rhyme that went the rounds. The names of three of the putative purchasers involved were Maximo, Endiquer and Mrs. Chapell. The rhymes went:

> "They seek him here, they seek him there,
> In fact, they seek him everywhere.
> Is he in Heaven? Is he in Hell?
> No he's in bed with Mrs. Chappell."

"*Eenie, meenie, Maximo,*
Catch Endiquer by the toe,
If he Quirkes let him go,
Lock, stock and barrel o."

The deal as far as I remember was eventually concluded successfully.

Bill Quirke continued to hunt when he had time and I recall him being a fearless man across country. He sadly dropped dead when hunting with the Ward Stag Hounds but no doubt it is the way he would have wished to go.

Another story my father told me is quite amusing: Sir Nugent Everard of Randalstown near Navan got an idea that he would import a couple of kangaroos and have a hunt after them. I don't' think he wished to kill or hurt them but thought that they had speed and would jump the fences very easily. All was arranged and a large crowd assembled at Randalstown for the novel hunt. The kangaroos were enlarged and apparently jumped a few fences then compounded, so ended that experiment.

Coming to shooting I also heard some quite amusing stories from my father. He owned a very good grouse shoot up on the Border between Tyrone and Donegal beside Pettigo. Going up to shoot there one time he had his great friend Jock Wilkinson with him. On their arrival at the border they were asked for the permits for their guns. Jock did not have one and customs officials said "No way can you bring your gun into the North." They talked for a while and Jock said "I'll let you into a secret, I have a horse running tomorrow and he will be a big price and will win." This horse was pretty useless and had run a few times, Jock didn't' even stay to see him run. The customs officials were talked into it and let him through. Amazingly the horse won at the very good odds and when they arrived back the customs men greeted them warmly for they all had put a few quid on the horse.

5. Farming, Shooting, Fishing, Golfing

On leaving school in 1939 I took over the running of Bellinter from my father. I certainly had no illusions as to the difficulty of doing the job successfully. Having reviewed the financial position I decided to wipe off the existing overdraft, which although not of immense proportions, still only left me with twelve pounds in the bank, an 800-acre demesne, 250 acres of which were woodland, and a certain amount of livestock.

As previously stated, in my grandfather's time there must have been between 10,000 and 15,000 acres in the whole estate with tenants in several counties. Under the Wyndham Act of 1903, landlords were obliged to sell out to their tenants for a fixed price. There was no option but to sell. Big houses were left without most of their sources of income so that it was difficult, if not economically possible, to keep them up.

When I took over, we had a ploughman, a herd and four men working on the farm. Each was paid ten shillings a week. That was the going rate at the time. There seemed only one possible method of survival and that entailed dispensing with some of the work force, which meant that I had to do a large part of the work myself.

I survived for about 8 years keeping dry stock and doing a small amount of tillage. I worked hard and I played hard and although I was continually pulling the devil by the tail, I enjoyed to the full a lot of hunting, shooting and fishing.

My shooting in this period consisted mainly of walking up snipe in the bogs, and rough shooting around the estate. Once or twice a year we had an organized pheasant shoot and although we did not get more than 50 or 60 birds, they flew wonderfully and took some shooting. There was always a party afterwards and it was usually late at night before that broke up. We also had a very good duck shoot under the house on the Boyne. We had hides built and got down to our stands before daylight and had some great mornings there. It is hard to believe that we would see three or four hundred duck at a time coming in. The sky at times was dark with them. How exciting it was! The snipe shooting was equally good. I used to shoot a lot with my cousin, George Malcolmson, and it was not uncommon to come home in the evening after a day on the bogs with 40 to 50 snipe.

David Ruttledge, a great friend of my father, had a vast amount of marvellous shooting near Ballinrobe in Mayo. My father and George Malcolmson brought me down a few times in the 1940s. It was undoubtedly the best shooting I have ever encountered. There were thousands of duck and snipe and a great number of woodcock. I even shot a deer one day. There was so much bog-land that you could shoot snipe all day without having to stop walking. David was bet one time that he would not shoot 100 snipe to his own gun in a day. He did it with time to spare.

I had many wonderful trips fishing and shooting with my cousin, George Malcolmson. On one occasion we were fishing on Lough Arrow and Lukie Massey and Lanny O'Keefe were also there. Soon after dinner in the hotel, Lanny disappeared to bed. Lukie said to George "What's wrong with that fellow always going to bed so early? Let's root him out." "Right", said George. When they got up to the bedroom door Lukie said to George "I'll open the door and you rush in and up-end him in the bed." This procedure was adopted but unknown to George, he had been sent into the bedroom of a parson and his wife. George accomplished his job all right and the parson and wife checked out of the hotel at 8 in the morning.

Lanny O'Keeffe, who was married to my first cousin, Dan Malcomson, was a keen fisherman. An exceedingly good man, he was somewhat vague at times. At a camp along Lough Sheelin one time he had his caravan down with us. I came up from the lake in my waders and Lanny gave me a can and asked "will you fill my oil lamp for me?" It was getting dark and I foolishly went up to put a little paraffin oil in the side filler while it was lighting. He had given me a can of petrol and the next thing I was engulfed in flames. Nobody ever ran for the lake quicker in waders with flames trailing behind them. I got into the lake in time and my goodness, I was lucky!

On another occasion in the 1940s when we were down at Ferrybridge on Lough Mask, Lanny arrived down by car at the caravan camp that was on the top of an incline down into the lake. We were chatting in the caravan and when I went out I said, "Where is your car, Lanny?" It transpired he had left it on the slope down to the lake, had not put the brake on properly and there it was almost submerged in the lake. I also was with Lanny on another fishing trip when he said "I must put some water in my car." He got a watering can and to my amazement took off the petrol cap and started pouring water into the petrol tank. I shouted that he must have a wonderful car if it runs on water. My father was fishing in a boat at Waterville one time with him when suddenly he was hooked by the ear. A few oaths from my father and Lanny said "Oh don't mind that, I hooked my gillie by the eye last week."

The Skane River, which runs through Bellinter, was very well stocked with lovely trout, running up to three quarters of a pound in weight. I had many happy days fishing there and, on occasions would bring back a bag of a dozen or more lovely fish. We also had the Boyne under the house. In the spring the salmon ran. In this period it was quite usual to get fish from 20 to 30 pounds in weight. A 12-pound fish was considered very small and you did not get them under that weight. The one drawback was that it was almost entirely bait fishing. I considered that form of fishing somewhat boring compared to fly-fishing. However, I did succeed in killing a certain number on the fly. With the drainage of the Boyne and drift netting at sea, the pattern has changed completely now.

The first of May was virtually the end of the fishing in the old days. Now you may catch fish down as low as 5 or 6 pounds right into September. I believe that this is partly due to the river being restocked with fish from the West where, of course, they run much smaller and later.

Lough Sheelin was at that time one of the finest trout-fishing lakes anywhere in the world. There was a tremendous rise of mayfly, which usually started at the end of May or beginning of June. My father used to have a camp on the lake with caravans and tents. We stayed down there for 2 to 3 weeks depending on how long the rise of fly lasted. We dapped the green drake during the daytime and on suitable evenings went after the trout with the dry fly or spent gnat. This was the most exciting form of fishing. Provided that there was a sufficient number of spent fly on the water, and it was reasonably calm, one would quite often see hundreds of large fish mopping them up. The skill was to get near enough to the fish without being seen, and then to try to place your fly in front of the path of your putative prey. The big fish seemed to be out in abundance and it was common to capture them at a weight of from 5 to 6 pounds; I have even caught them up to 7 pounds.

Unfortunately, my father's records have been lost, but I do remember we used to get 200 trout or more, and what seems almost unbelievable now is that we used to throw back any fish under 2 pounds weight! They were beautiful trout and played very hard. I vividly remember the first I ever caught on the dap. I had him on for a short time when the top of my rod broke. My father quickly managed to tie my line onto his and then cut mine free. He played the fish for a long time. The difficulty being that the top of my rod kept hitting the trout on the nose and off he would go again. We eventually landed him and retrieved my rod top. He was 5 pounds weight, a pretty good fish. This period was the highlight of the fishing but angling on the lake has since gone into a steady decline.

The camp used to move down to Lough Mask in September. This is a lovely, unspoiled lake. At that time of the year it was particularly good for dapping the grasshopper and daddy long legs. We used to catch a lot of fish but they did not, on average, run near as large as the Sheelin trout. There are, however, very large trout, which if caught, are nearly always taken trolling the bait. There is an interesting trout that has a gizzard and called a gillaroo, that is only found in Loughs Mask and Melvin.

It was in this period that I started to play golf. This was to be expected as my father had founded the Bellinter Park Golf Club on the estate in 1923. This is now the self-styled *Royal Tara Golf Club*. There had been a golf club in Navan before then. I think that it was located on the site of the present Rugby club grounds. The club folded up sometime in the very early twenties. My father, along with some of his good friends such as Jack Spicer, Tom Noonan, Jim McQuillan and Jimmy Lyons, came together to discuss the possibility of forming a new golf club. It was my father's idea as he had the land at Castletown Tara that was suitable for such a venture. The entrance to the club was the main entrance to Bellinter in the old days. However, all contributed in their own way and Bellinter Park Golf Club came into being. This was in 1923. Sixty acres of land were allocated for the laying out of the course that, at that time, was a nine-hole course. They got the thing going and built a fairly basic clubhouse with a corrugated iron roof. There was a bit of a bar that served bottled ale and stout as well as spirits. There was no catering or fancy drinks in those days. Mrs. Fagan, who lived nearby, came in to look after things. She must have been there for nearly forty years. When I got married in 1947 she was still there and was there for a long time afterwards.

6. Racing during the War

DURING the war years, from 1939 to 1945, we used to have the supply column of the army camping in the woods during the summer when they were on manoeuvres. We also had several aeroplanes from the Air Corps landing on the 120-acre lawn in front of the house with the officers camping on the other side of the house. All the officers were made honorary members of the golf club. My goodness, what parties went on in the clubhouse! One day George Malcolmson arrived down with his pony and trap. Some of the boys said "Bring the pony in and give him a drink". This was done and a bottle of Guinness was poured into an army hat and given to the pony. Great laughter arose until an army officer called Gilleece discovered that it was his hat. He had been heavy weight boxing champion in the army and was not too pleased. He had a slight argument with George and in fun they faced up to each other. George had been a good boxer at Trinity College, Dublin and proceeded to hit a bit too hard and knocked two of Gilleece's front teeth out. However, it all ended amicably.

Although at that time I did not have very much of an association with horse racing, I kept a few point-to-pointers. The best one I had was a mare called *Tonight's The Night*. It was rather amusing that there were three other horses running at the same time called, respectively, *Wait and See*, *Do It Again* and *Time Will Tell*.

I rode in only a few point-to-point races as I was always too heavy and my ability to race-ride was not great. My younger sister, Stella, was a very capable rider and rode a few winners for me. One of the horses that I had at the time was called *King's Shilling* that Stella rode for me at a point-to-point at Dalystown and won at thirty-three to one. Oh, we had a great day of it after that.

Waring Willis was to ride *King's Shilling* for me in a good race at Punchestown. At the time Cecil Brabazon was training it. We thought that it had a good chance of winning. At the last minute, Archie Willis, Waring's father, told Waring that he had to ride a horse for Lord Glentoran. In his northern accent, Archie said, "The wee boy has to ride for the lord." Waring was a top rider at the time so Cecil Brabazon was furious. Anyway, we had to get another rider and off they went. One of the fences was a wall with furze bushes in front of it. The horse thought that it was an ordinary fence and that it could brush through it but wasn't and it couldn't. The horse and rider fell when they looked like winning. I sold the horse afterwards and did all right on the transaction.

At that time the courses were all ditches and banks. It was inevitable, however, that this would have to change. Horses were becoming more valuable and too many were getting hurt and killed.

I used to enjoy going to some of the holiday race meetings in the summer. Galway, Listowel and Tramore all had a wonderful holiday atmosphere and we really enjoyed ourselves. Aubrey Brabazon, my first cousin, was very often with us. He rode the winner of the Galway Plate on two occasions and won many top races both here and across the water, including the Gold Cup three times and the Champion Hurdle twice.

During the war years it was almost impossible to get enough petrol to go any distance. Not to be denied our annual caravan and tent expedition to the Galway races, my father put a further two front wheels on the old caravan and rigged up shafts to the front of it so that it could have been pulled by a horse. An old pony cart and a trap were also acquired. Thus equipped, the whole shebang set off for Galway about a week before the races were due to start. My father and mother used to travel down to Galway by rail a few days after we had set off in the caravan and carts.

Aunt Gladys and the younger generation did the driving of the caravan, cart and trap. We also brought a couple of bicycles with us so that some of us could go ahead to find a suitable place where we could stay the night and put out our horses. I remember that there was a lovely priest in Kilbeggan who arranged for us to have the use of a field by the town and who gave us a first class welcome. We covered about twenty-five miles a day on a wonderfully leisurely trip.

It seems hard to visualize such a get-up today when one sees the amount of traffic on the roads. It seems incredible now that our cavalcade passed through big towns like Athlone, Ballinasloe and Galway City. We had a bad scare on one trip when Aunt Gladys became quite ill in the caravan. We were very concerned and set out to try to find a doctor, but without success. We tended to her in the best way we could. After two or three days she recovered and on we went to Galway. En route we met many interesting people who helped us and entertained us. No doubt, we were a source of entertainment to them also.

On reaching Galway we were given permission to strike camp and to put out our horses on a small farm at Gentian Hill, just beyond Salthill. The Seymours, a well-known family in the Galway area, owned the farm and were very kind to us. We used our bicycles to go into the city, which wasn't far away. One night Aubrey Brabazon, my cousin, and I were out enjoying the fun in the city. We probably had drunk a little too much in our pursuit of jollity. When we decided to return to the camp it was dark and quite late. Unknown to us the owners had put a bar across the entrance to the field. I was in front of Aubrey with no light on my bicycle; I hit the bar and was thrown over it and landed a few yards ahead on the ground. Fortunately, I wasn't hurt. It was about 6 o'clock in the morning when we climbed into our bunks in our tent. At about 7 o'clock, Uncle Cecil, Aubrey's father, looked in and said "Good lad," to Aubrey, "You've had a good sleep." Aubrey was riding in the Galway Plate later that day.

On another occasion Deirdre Sheppard, Ann Chute and a young boy appeared unexpectedly at our camp and told us that they were in a bit of a fix as that they could not find anywhere to stay the night. Every place was full up. We took pity on them and told them that we would put them up somehow. My father and mother along with Cecil Brabazon and Aunt Gladys as well as Lelia, I think, were sleeping in the old caravan, which really had only three proper bunks. Anyway, that night the two girls, Deirdre and Ann, also slept there. I don't know how they all fitted in. The boy slept on the floor of our tent between Aubrey and me. However, we were all in holiday mood and had great fun.

Before the war we used to travel to Tramore and to Listowel for the races when petrol wasn't scarce but those places were too far away for our horse-drawn outfit. On one evening we were dining in the Majestic Hotel in Tramore. The place was packed. Geoffrey Gilpin, who was very often up to some devilment or other, was also dining at the time. Suddenly he shouted "Rat, rat, there he goes." There was consternation. There were women up on the tables, screaming. Every now and then Geoffrey shouted, "There he goes." The damage caused to crockery and furniture must have been considerable. I don't know how Geoffrey got himself out of that scrape.

On another occasion at the Listowel races we rented a cottage at Ballybunion. A great friend of ours, and a character, Booie Fetherstonhaugh, was down there at the time and took a girl out for a walk on the beach. There are well-known caves there, which one may enter when the tide is out. Booie, with something other than horse racing on his mind, went into a cave with the girl. Shortly afterwards the pair realised that they were almost cut off by the incoming tide. They got out with water up to their chests and were lucky to have escaped. That cooled Booie's ardour!

Racing at this period was undergoing a considerable clean up. It may be interesting to relate a few stories told to me by my father as to what used to happen earlier in the 20th century. A large number of races in those days was fixed among the riders. David Ruttledge was the official judge at most of the meetings. The judge's box was very often just standing on four legs. At a particular meeting in the south a certain very well known rider and trainer had a large bet on his horse. He was not entirely confident as to the genuineness of the horse. However, before the race he hired two tough lads. They sawed two of the legs of the judge's box fairly well through and then leaned against it to support it. If the horse was winning they were to stay there. As the horse was being well beaten they walked away from the box whereupon it collapsed and away went David. The race was null and void as there was no judge in the box!

Leslie Brabazon, a brother of my uncle Cecil, had trained horses in Bellinter, where there were very good gallops. He brought a horse to Listowel that he thought would win but the horse was not a good jumper. He did not like the last fence at all so he decided the night before to throw it into the River Feale, which flows alongside the racetrack! I understand that the horse did not win anyway so that it was labour in vain.

In his younger days before he had been injured, my father was not a very accomplished race rider and used to be put up on the non-triers! Leslie Brabazon had a very good horse with which he had planned to have a big betting coup at Galway. He ran a few weeks beforehand at Bellewstown and Leslie's instructions to my father were that the horse was not to win on any account. The horse was a hard puller and it became obvious to my father that there was no way that he could stop him. There were only three horses in the race. There were two sharp turns on each end of the course so he decided that the only thing he could do was to go straight on at one end and into a heap of gorse bushes. To his consternation, when he turned around he found the other two horses with him. They had a discussion and it transpired that none of them were off. Cecil Brabazon, who was riding one of the horses, decided that he had better go on and win, which he did. My father was seriously reprimanded and fined but the third jockey, who stated that my father had carried him out, although a considerable way behind, was disqualified from riding at races for quite a while. There were other incidents of fences having been burnt and other sorts of skulduggery. It was no wonder that the conduct of racing had to be cleaned up.

7. Hunting

HUNTING had become my first love in my sporting world. My first hunt was in 1928 when I was seven years old. It was a meet from Bellinter House with the Meath Hunt. I had a very good pony, one of the many that I had the pleasure to ride when I was child. When Bill Quirke retired in 1942 I became joint master with Lukie. At that time I was the youngest master of hounds in the country. This position I still hold albeit with other joint masters down through the years.

In the early nineteenth century many packs of hounds came together to form the Meath Hounds, but the Bellinter Harriers, as they were then known, remained independent and still survived. An article in an edition of 1914 of *British Hunts and Huntsmen* described the Tara Harriers as "one of the best harrier packs in the Kingdom, consisting of nineteen and a half couples of eighteen-inch, pure bred hounds, which hunt two days a week over the largest harrier country in the British Isles."

Records of the Hunt show that in the early nineteen hundreds there was a dearth of hares. In my early days I remember seeing only two or three hares in a day. At present, the position has changed and it is not uncommon to see several hares in the same field.

Having taken over hunting the hounds I became more and more involved and interested. I look back now to that period as the best and most exciting hunting I have enjoyed in my lifetime. There was less wire, less tillage, far less sheep and virtually no intensive farming like we have today.

Farmers were very tolerant and sporting in those days and one could stay with the hounds in a good hunt whereas, it is very much harder to do so now.

At that time I hunted the hounds in the Navan country and Lukie continued in the Trim-Enfield region. We could not go very far a field because we had no cars on the road and we had to hack to meets. This entailed some long hacks for me but the big difficulty we had was getting to the other end, which involved journeys of twenty miles or more. The difficulty was overcome by the wonderful efforts of our kennel huntsman, Christy Dowdall. He would set out on his bicycle on Sunday afternoon and ride to Perth House, over twenty miles away, with the pack of hounds following him. It seems almost incredible to me that he did this regularly and only once in all of those journeys did he lose the hounds. When the hounds were fed, enclosed and safe, Lukie and Christy would take off to the local shebeen on their bikes and survived their journeys home without doing themselves damage.

The hounds hunted the next day, and after retiring to the pub for a few jars at the end of the day, Christy set off for home. It was on one of those journeys that the pack got lost. It was snowing heavily and there was a few inches of snow on the ground. Just as they were nearing Laracor a fox crossed the road. The hounds sped off in pursuit. Christy could hear them for miles as they hunted the fox and could do nothing about it. Christy came home with no hounds that evening. "Never mind", I said, "They will be all home tomorrow." Next day there was no sight or sound of the hounds so that Christy had to set off to look for them. To my amazement he returned that evening still with no hounds. "A pack of hounds just cannot disappear," I said, so off again he went the following day. He found them about five miles from where they took up the fox's scent, lying on a big bank. A dead beast was in a ditch nearby and the pack had devoured a great deal of it and was full and quite content to stay there. However, Christy gathered them together and brought them back to the kennels.

Lukie and I decided shortly after the war had ended that we needed some new blood. We had heard a lot about the Kerry Beagles, and as then we had an old hound van, we decided to go down south to see what we could find. We stayed in Killarney on the first night and set off the following morning for Cahirciveen, where we had some contacts. Having spent all of that day travelling around to various houses, we were eventually told to go to a certain pub in the town and anyone around who wished to sell a hound would be there that evening. All went well at first and we purchased a few hounds. Drinks came up fast and furious and the whole procedure became like a cabaret show! Hounds were produced every few minutes. We would say: "No, we don't care about that one", and so it went on. I am quite certain that as more and more drink was consumed that the same hounds were being shown again and again until we accepted them. We finished up with five and a half couple and returned to Killarney for the night.

We arrived back to Bellinter next evening and put our hounds in the kennels. Next morning, in spite of there being a high wall around the run, there was only one of our Kerry hounds left: My father told me that when he got hounds from there that he used to buy only pups and young, un-entered hounds. We had bought old hounds that had never been kennelled and were always running free. They must have been great jumpers!

Unfortunately, our troubles did not end there, as we would periodically get word of hound bitches with pups in ditches and various other places; those hounds did not know us and were wild. It took quite a while and the payment of some compensation before that business was ended.

The following appeared in a local newspaper (The Kerryman?) regarding our visit to Kerry: *Iveragh, traditional home of the Kerry Beagle was honoured over the weekend by a visit from two members of one of the oldest established hunting packs in the land. The visitors, Messrs. G. Briscoe and H. Massey, joint masters of the Tara Harriers, a hunt with a history dating back to the middle of the eighteenth century. The purpose of the Meath sportsmen's visit was to purchase a number of Kerry*

Beagles with a view to infusing new blood into their own patriarchal pack, the ranks of which had been impaired through inbreeding over a long number of years. Mr. Briscoe told me that the reason the hunt selected the south Kerry strain for the rejuvenation of their pack was that his father, Mr. C. Briscoe, (former master) had purchased some Iveragh hounds over thirty years ago which gave performances on the rolling plains of the Royal County that are still reverently recalled. Speaking of the hounds which he had been shown during his visit, Mr. Briscoe said that they were the finest specimens that he had ever seen and that there was not one of them that the Tara Hunt would not be proud to own, but he had to adhere to his terms of reference and could only purchase four couple. It is the earnest hope of all in Iveragh that these eight hounds will worthily uphold the prestige of the Kerry Beagle in their new environment. During their stay the visitors were chaperoned by huntsman, Mr. Corcoran, out in Cahirciveen and entertained by members of the hunt.

Apart from hunting the harriers, I regularly hunted with the Meath Foxhounds. The master at that time was Nancy Connell who was a wonderful lady, and not only was she master of the Meaths, but was for many years master of the North Kildare Harriers. My friend for many years, Colonel Charles Cameron, hunted the Meaths for a while before the war and, on his return from the war, was joint master and huntsman for many years.

It is remarkable how things have changed. When I first became a member of the Meath hunt Committee in 1944 nothing less than the Shelbourne Hotel in Dublin would do as a venue for our meetings. I drove up there with my bowler hat on and in a pin-stripe suit. We had a room to ourselves with servants laid on to bring us drinks and food. It was a very pukka occasion. At present we hold our meetings over a pub in Watergate Street in Navan.

During those years I used to spend a few days from time to time in Cork with my great friend, Dick Dwyer. I went down for a hunt ball, hunting and shooting. The snipe and woodcock were very plentiful and we had some marvellous bags of 30 to 40 snipe and a good number of woodcock in a day's shooting. It is not easy to get those kinds of bags at the present day.

The hunting in Cork was really wonderful and I had some of my best days of my life with the United Foxhounds. This was all made possible for me owning to the kindness and generosity of my dear friend, Dick Dwyer. He periodically asked me down to his lovely home, Mayfield, beside Cork City, to stay and to hunt, shoot and go to their hunt ball. He had me mounted with top class horses and his hospitality, and indeed, that of all his Cork friends, was quite unforgettable.

I don't believe that I ever had a bad day with the United and I seemed to bring them luck every time I went down. I remember one day in particular. We met at Watergrasshill and our first draw was Ballygeorge. We found a stout fox there and ran a fast six-mile point to lair, Glen Brown's Covert. I was very proud to have been presented with the mask by Freeman, the huntsman. The marathon was yet to come. We found again in lair and we ran, I understand, over twenty miles in to Muskerry country. Several things stick in my mind in this hunt. The master, Tiny Halliman, who rode at twenty stone, finished the hunt, which was a wonderful achievement. I was quite amazed to see Willie O'Grady ride the hunt to the end having broken a leather early on. He was an exceptional horseman and a wonderful man to ride to hounds. I don't believe that I could ride a field without stirrup leathers let alone big, high banks that one encounters down there. Two other people who were very hard to follow were Peg Watt and Pat Hogan, both of whom hunted mainly in Limerick but who were very often out with the United.

The following is a piece of verse that I wrote at that time, In *memory of a great day with the United Foxhounds at a meet at Whitechurch, 27th. February 1945.*

Once again my brave sports to Cork City we go
To compete in the sport that was stopped by the snow
We rode the best hunt that I've ever seen
The fox was a champion, the pace was full steam.

With the master[1] at Whitechurch we have a few rounds
As gallant a man as ever rode to the hounds
With a weight that would break Prince Regent in two
He'll ride with the best and beat them too.

1. Tiny Hallinan

Now Dick[2] is away with hounds like a hare
It's a good man will be with him and remain there
Though riding the Yank as hard as I knew
I could seldom get better than his back view

2. Dick Dwyer

Of Jack[3] and his horse they all speak with awe
If you can, keep behind him, you won't get before
I've ridden with many great men to the hounds
But Dick and himself would get the crowns

3. Jack Dwyer

Ladies should be first in this poem, 'tis true
For at the head of the hunt you'll find Eithne[4] and Coo[5]
Over banks and ditches in south or north
Great riders, great goers, true lovers of the sport

4. Eithne Dwyer
5. Cooleen Dwyer

Good luck to you Cooleen, not for charm alone,
Do I love and admire you, as you have always known
A great lover of hunting you have always been
And for that, if no other, I'd make you my queen

Et had the bad luck to break up her horse
While going like a train, I needn't mention, of course
But that is the luck of the chase as we know
That some are stopped short while others may go

Mrs. Dwyer[6] is the next, as cool as could be
Riding on the banks, a pleasure to see
She warned me just once a few yards down there's a gate
But I didn't listen and there met my fate   6. Dick Dwyer's wife

Bold Charlie[7] o'er the country is transported with ease
Like the daring young man on the flying trapeze
He flew just too hard at a couple of places
But was there to the fore at the end of both chases   7. Charlie Dwyer

The most courageous of all was Fez[8] we know
In spite of nine falls, he still had a go
Till exhausted and plastered from head to feet
He retired from the contest to the place of the meet   8. Fez Byrne

To be concussed and merry both at the same time
Is a feat of endurance, the rest will not rhyme
His joie de vivre coming home in the trap
Was not suggestive of so many a crack

Mimi[9] got a fall right into the muck
And was paddling around like a young duck
I came to the rescue, it was a pleasure, of course
To put such a sport back onto her horse   9. Mimi Hallinan

Eamonn[10] got a fall while up in the front
Just before the last check, near the end of the hunt
His prayers must have been very strong indeed
To hold up the hunt while he recovered his steed   10. Eamonn Rohan

Phyl[11] came to grief in a large ravine
The horse went right down and couldn't be seen
After much strenuous work he emerged from the deep
But the hounds were past catching except in a jeep   11. Phyl Rohan

The squire[12] at the meet thought of business first
By supporting the firm to assuage his thirst
He rode across county with judicious haste
One result, the horse was sold, at the end of the chase

12. Squire Murphy

Who's that to the fore wherever you look?
Tis Willie O'Grady if I'm not mistook
He's a devil to go whenever he's out
Be it north or east or west or south

There's Peg[13] going strong, a hard rider too
She gets across country just like a U2
O'er the same fence as I she came a hard crack
But was soon up and after that hard-running pack

13. Peg Watt

Of Timmy Moloney, I get hard to place
The things that happened to the noble ace
I know he got one fall in front of me
For that my evil eye was there to see

And now here comes Declan[14] arriving in state
By atrocious bad luck he was to soon meet his fate
The horse he did stumble and send him head first
In a blooming bog hole, what could have been worse?

14. Declan Dwyer

But Dodo[15] is there to the fore all right
Keeping the hounds well within sight
There's no stopping the ladies down in the south
They're all devils to go, of that there's no doubt

15. Dodo Dwyer

Glen[16] has arrived at the meet today
Decked out in splendour to join in the fray
Another hard rider I need hardly add
For down in that country there isn't one bad

16. Glen Brown

There's the great lady I only know by name
But I very soon spotted she was of hunting fame
Clare Mahony, I speak of, and speak with awe
Such a lion-hearted lady I've not seen before

To leave out Freeman, the huntsman, would indeed be absurd
He's a good man with hounds and they hark to his word
He up with his hounds you are certain to see
As any good huntsman must always be

Now this was Stella's[17] first visit to Cork
By Jove, she enjoyed it, you should hear her talk
A toast to the health of the Dwyers is now nigh
We pray for our friendship to last till we die   17. Stella Briscoe

Of the hunt I can't write for I know not the way
That very hard fox ran on the mem'rable day
With proudness I say if someone should ask
A most wonderful day and I have the mask

And that is the end of my story, I fear
May it bring back happy memories, full of good cheer
But one thing remains, a warm-hearted call
Good luck to the Dwyers, good luck to you all

The hunt balls in Cork were very lively and great fun especially with a number of lovely and attractive girls around. Dick Dwyer's daughter, Ethne, married my cousin, the late Aubrey Brabazon. They had a long and happy life together and had a most attractive family.

Hunting continued well with the Taras and we had a lot of fun and enjoyment and we were particularly blessed in having a very good and sporting lot of members.

Our very good friend, Avia Riddle-Martin, who lived in the Ballivor area in the seventies and eighties, has been very good to the Tara Harriers. Andy Elliott, who was a well-known farmer and a great supporter of hunting, also lived in that locality. He was a bachelor and lived in an old thatched house a couple of miles from the village. We would meet at McLoughlin's public house and, upon entering the premises, Andy would be there dispensing drinks to everyone. He was a very generous man to the hunt followers, all of whom were his friends. When Leslie Johnson went "warning" the farmers with him for a few days' hunting in the area, they might "warn" a couple of farmers and then retire to his thatched cottage amongst the pots and pans and spend the rest of the day consuming a bottle of whiskey. "Don't worry about them," he would say. "I know them all and everything will be alright." He was right. They were great and most agreeable farmers around there.

I was looking for a good young horse to buy and Andy said that he had just the animal. I went over to see him. Andy took the horse out and proceeded to jump quite a formidable fence off the road outside his house, which was fair enough but there was a telephone pole with a stay wire on it and he jumped between the two. I promptly bought the horse that turned out to be brilliant and one of the best horses I ever had. Andy was a farmer of considerable means and bred and sold horses for show jumping. I never go to Ballivor meets without thinking of Andy, who passed away some years ago.

We have a very good ambassador for the hunt up in Bailieborough called Wilkie Lytle. He is a farmer and is very well known around the Cavan area. An excellent judge of a horse, he has put many good ones through his hands, and indeed used to buy some of the horses for the British mounted police. He is so well known up there that he is practically indispensable to the Tara Harriers.

I well remember when hunting in the Tierworker area one day in the 1980s when the hounds were blamed for having caused the death of a calf. Wilkie went to see the owner of the calf who told him that the calf had been a very valuable animal as that it had been sired by a top bull through the agency of artificial insemination. In order to validate this claim, Wilkie enquired at the A.I. office to discover that the farmer had never had a cow inseminated by them. Next time we met at Tierworker after the hunt we decided that we would go down to see the farmer and give him some compensation. Having had a few drinks we went down and knocked on the door. A woman came out and we asked to see the farmer. "He's just after dying," she said. We retired rapidly.

The following year when we were again hunting around Tierworker we were having a nice hunt when we came upon a man shouting and roaring at us to get out. He was brandishing a slash hook and had a shovel on the ground. We beat a retreat but unfortunately, one of our members, Johnnie Clements, fell into a big ditch full of muck. The angry man was bearing down upon him rapidly when Wilkie shouted at him: "You had better be careful; the last fellow who fell out with this hunt dropped dead shortly afterwards." Johnnie emerged from the ditch covered in black mud and made his escape.

I was hunting the hounds one day in the eighties and we had our meet at Bective village. We had completed our day's hunting and were returning to the village when, coming around the corner, I was confronted by army tanks with their guns pointing at me, and soldiers doing the same and shouting "Take cover, the *Border Fox* will be here at any minute!" I do remember in my amazement saying that we were just hunting hares. Since the '*Border Fox's*' name was O'Hare, this struck me afterwards as a rather bizarre statement for me to have made. However, it was a spur of the moment reaction. Anyway, there was some consternation on my part, as I didn't see how I was going to take cover whilst on horseback and a pack of hounds trailing behind.

Afterwards I heard that the notorious 'Border Fox' was trying to escape across the River Boyne. And that it was suspected that he would try to make the crossing at Bective Bridge.

My daughter and son-in-law live at Asigh beside the old railway bridge over the river. This is the one I had purchased from C.I.E. It was thought that O'Hare might have escaped over that bridge, as it had not been manned.

Hunting one day from a meet at Moynalty, we found a good running hare which ran up Screebogge Hill. Joan Mullins and I jumped a drop fence with wire in it and then found that we were wired in. Hounds were hunting hard and I said that there was nothing for it but to jump four strands of wire. I rode at it, mounted on *Compactus,* a well-known, former National Hunt horse. He took the fence with him but fell in the process and I found myself nearly compacted on the ground under his belly. He was lashing out trying to get up but I was stuck under him preventing his legs getting to the ground. How long this lasted I do not know but I remember Joan Mullins coming to my assistance and not finding the answer. Eventually we got disentangled with no damage done and remounted, caught up with the hounds and finished the hunt.

One day out hunting we set off from the Bailieborough Co-op and went into a lovely part of the country. There was plenty of cover with furze bushes, small bogs and woods but not a sign of either a fox or a hare. We had just about used up all of our country that had been 'warned' and I was resigned to going home. Suddenly, there was a great cry from a gorse bush and I followed them on. To my dismay, when I got to the far end I saw a large cat with the hounds in full cry after it. Fortunately for the cat there was a lone holly tree in the area up which it scrambled to safety. I was severely embarrassed when the field arrived and saw the cat up the tree and the hounds all baying at the bottom.

Robinstown is one our best meets. One day, Terry Dowdall, who was our huntsman, asked me as I was following around in the car, if I would keep an eye on a very large flock of sheep beside Willie Smith's farm. I walked out into a field beside them and next thing heard the hounds hunting towards me. I thought that I had better rush on and get near the sheep. Unknown to me, I met a large, muddy deep ditch full of water over which I could not see a way. Anyway, I took off my boots and trousers and rolled up my shirt and took to the stream. I waded across with the water up to my neck. Upon reaching the other side I just had my trousers on before all the followers appeared, and I proceeded to act as shepherd to the flock.

At this time Avia gave a lawn meet for the Tara Harriers at her home at Ballivor. This was quite a meet and a large crowd assembled. The plan was that Andy Elliot would arrange to run a drag from near the meet. The liquid refreshment flowed and when I announced that we were moving off I said to Andy "Where do we start?" Believe it or not he had forgotten to organize his runners for the drag. This entailed a long delay before the move off by which time many of our contestants were quite under the weather! However we eventually attempted to make a start and with great hilarity, certain well-known followers had great difficulty in getting on to their horses and, when mounted, had great difficulty in staying there. I laid on the hounds and we were getting on well for a couple of miles when there was a check and a voice came from the bottom of a ditch "Be Jove, you've caught me," said the man who was laying the drag.

I had an appointment to meet our Bishop in Trim at 6 o'clock that evening after the meet and, in anticipation of a delay, I brought a change of clothes. This was fine until I discovered that I had forgotten to put in a pair of shoes. I enquired of Avia would she have any men's shoes around as I could not very well meet the Bishop in my hunting boots. "Where the hell would I get those?" she asked. Charlie Bird was over from the States and was at the meet. I was wondering where he was and was informed that he had gone up to have a lie down for a while. I crept up to the room where he was sleeping and managed to remove his shoes without waking him so I was then all set to meet the Bishop. Apparently there was quite a bit of consternation when Charlie woke up and could not find his shoes and no one knew I had lifted them. That was quite a day.

Hunting continued successfully and Commander Collard retired as joint-master and left Ireland for The Isle of Man. His place was taken over by David Wilkinson and shortly afterwards Lorraine joined us in the mastership. We now had my cousin, Susie Lannigan O'Keeffe, my nephew, Henry Smith, Lorraine, David and myself. It may seem that we might have too many masters but owing to the increased pressure in running a hunt that situation is the norm with many packs in order to spread the load. David opened up considerably more country in the Longwood end and we had some excellent meets at Broadford, Carbery and Ballyboggin. Those places are in Kildare Hunt country but had not been hunted for years by them. We got a very good reception from the many farmers around there.

My very good friend for many years, Waring Willis, is buried in the graveyard on the top of the Hill of Tara, a lovely spot to be laid to rest. A few months after his death in 1987 we were hunting there and got a hare on foot with hounds screaming right up to the cemetery wall with the hare in full sight. On reaching the wall, within a few yards of Waring's grave, there was complete silence. I cast around everywhere but could not get any line, which was extraordinary as it was open country and there was no cover of any sort. It was quite uncanny and I often wondered where that hare could have gone. Perhaps it was a spiritual tribute to a great character and sportsman and one with whom I had been initiated into hunting hounds in our school days at Portora.

In 1988 I decided that it was time for me to hand over the horn to Terry Dowdall. I felt that I was slowing up and not doing justice to a good pack of hounds and also being a bit of a menace to our followers in falling off into ditches, and so on. I continued hunting and Terry did a good job in carrying on good sport. A presentation was made to him at the opening meet in 1989 of a gold watch in appreciation of 25 years service to the hunt. He was a hard worker, whose tasks included the collection and the skinning of farm animals that had died on farms and also the feeding of their flesh to our hounds. The removal of such animals from farmland is a service we give our farmers, with whom we have had a very good relationship, and one that is important to maintain.

In 1992 I was told that Lorraine was planning a big party at our opening meet to celebrate my 50 years mastership and also most of that period as huntsman of the pack. Such a party! A massive tent was erected at Asigh and over 300 people were invited to a sit- down dinner, presentation and dancing. A disaster almost struck; but for the will of God I might never have made it. A few days before, I was riding a big four-year-old horse that we had just bought and I went out for a run with the hounds before the opening. I caught my foot in a bush on jumping a small fence and I lost my iron. I was struggling to get it back when the horse turned sharply and put me off balance. If I had fallen straight off I would have been all right but unfortunately I hung on and he took off at full gallop. I did not remember for a while what happened as I fell on my head and was knocked out. Fortunately, my good friend, Austin Darragh, was out with us and pronounced that I was fit to be moved to hospital. It transpired that I had broken two bones in my neck and broken my wrist. I made it to the party where I was presented with a magnificent painting of myself on my old hunter, *Robinstown*, with Terry and the hounds in the background. The famous painter, Peter Curling, was the artist. I was trussed up like a chicken with a collar around my neck and my arm in plaster. Nevertheless, I made it and the party went on until the early hours of the morning.

Unfortunately that was the end of my riding career. I tried to carry on but had not much movement in my neck and my balance was not good. However, I had a great innings and am still maintaining a great interest in the hunt and remain a joint-master and follow all the hunts around in the car. The hunting carried on pretty well until the middle of the 1999-2000 season when Terry got considerable trouble with his back and was unable to finish the season. Henry Smith came in to fill the breech and hunted them most successfully for the remainder of the season. Terry's daughter, Sabine, who had been doing our horses for several years, came into help Terry with the hounds and did a great job. It was quite obvious that poor Terry was a sick man at the start of the 2000-2001 season and he could not carry on. It was very sad when he passed away on 15th April 2001, having fought a brave battle against cancer for a considerable time. He had been 37 years with the hunt. Henry took over hunting the hounds with Sabine, our kennel huntsman. They did a great job and certainly gave us an excellent season. We were most fortunate to get Jessica Magnier, daughter of the late Waring Willis, and Abi Hill to come in as joint-masters to replace Susie Lannigan O'Keeffe and David Wilkinson who retired, having given great service and who had put in many years of hard work.

We are delighted that David Wilkinson has returned. The position in 2005 is that the masters are, Lorraine McDowell, Henry Smith, Abi Hill, David Wilkinson and myself.

For many years Jessica has hosted the hunter trials on her farm at Skryne. It is a superb course and a most popular venue, which brings big crowds every year and greatly helps the hunt funds. Unfortunately it cannot continue, as the proposed new motorway will swallow up part of it. It is hoped for the present to hold the hunter trials in Henry Smith's farm at Donabate.

Our joint point-to-point race meeting with the Meath Hunt has been a resounding success for years which is largely due to the generosity of John Fowler in not only giving the loan of the beautiful course at Rahinston but also being instrumental in doing the lion's share of the work both by himself and his staff.

Many people ask me why we have a joint point-to-point race and why not one each? This came about in the 1970s when we held our point-to-point in Dunsany. I was approached by the Meath Hunt to know if we would let them come in with us, as they had no course, Navan racecourse having been closed to point-to-pointing. Our two packs had always had a very close relationship from my grandfather's time, and as I had been chairman of the Meaths I took it upon myself to agree. It has been a most successful amalgamation both socially and financially.

It is worth recording that to my knowledge we were the first point-to-point in Ireland to use portable fences when the Turf Club permitted point-to-points to race between the flags. Vincent Eivers, one of our great supporters, was secretary of our point-to-point over the banks at Dalystown. When banks became too dangerous for the increasing value of the horses, the Turf Club amended their rules. Vincent said "You can have a course on my land at Roriston and I shall make the fences". It was remarkable how he designed the first movable fences and a great credit must go to him. The more modern type is based on his original design. A team from the hunt went out on the bogs to cut birch for filling them. What a job, it nearly killed us getting to roads to load trailers. However, it all came about and we had our first pont-to-point over moveable fences in Roriston in 1960. It may be of interest to note that in the olden times the Meaths' annual point-to-point races were held at Tara where the course was of two laps around the summit of the hill.

Having had so much enjoyment and happiness in my life from hunting and particularly from hunting hounds I feel somewhat sad that this wonderful sport has been under attack from misguided and misinformed people who have no knowledge whatsoever of the sport. It is a field and country sport and I see no reason why these unattractive *antis* come out trying to stop something of which they have no knowledge and which is so dear to many farmers and country people. Do they not realize that they are putting many peoples' livelihoods in the country at risk? The funds that the *antis* have amassed from anti-social and misguided people are used to pay young agitators to go around and harass innocent people doing no harm to anyone. They have made a devastating impression on the hunts in England. We are very lucky here in that the law does not protect them the way they are protected in England. There they have attacked and abused people on their horses and if any retaliation took place it was always the horseman who was prosecuted and judged at fault. Since early 2005, foxhunting with a pack of hounds has been out-lawed in England and Wales.

I well remember the first time the Tara Harriers got harassment from a bus load of scruffy young people from, I gathered, Liverpool. I was grounded from a fall and following around in my car. I heard a horn blowing and shouting going on and did not cotton on to what was happening. I came up a hill and saw this scruffy group putting things on the ground and blowing horns. Fortunately I was in an area where I knew the farmers very well. I called, "Come here!" A few came up to the road and I asked "Have you got the owner of this farm's permission to go out on his land?" They shied away and I said "Come here, I want two or three to come with me to the farmer." They refused and I said "Alright, if you don't get to hell out of here we shall sue you for trespass." They boarded their bus and disappeared. The following day they appeared at a meet of the Meath Foxhounds. However, I had alerted the master of that hunt the previous evening that *antis* were around.

A famous character called Ned Cash, king of the itinerants, and owner of many horses, got the message. When they appeared at the meet Ned and some of his pals beat up a couple of them and they retired in disorder. Next they decided to go down and attack the Ballymacads that were hunting near Oldcastle. The Ballymacads had been alerted. At their meet, the Ballymacads parked a powerful tractor out of sight. When the *antis* left their bus to demonstrate, the tractor came around quickly, hooked up a chain to the bus and towed it out into the middle of a 50-acre ploughed field and left it there. History does not relate how they got out of that. Thankfully, we have not seen any *antis* since that time.

There are of course many other things that adversely affect us with our hunting. A few years ago some insignificant person who was out shooting fell over an old plough on a farmer's land and broke his leg. He claimed compensation from the farmer, which was of course quite ridiculous. However, this had huge implications for hunt clubs throughout the country. Many of them produced a waiver to be signed by the hunt followers exonerating the farmer from any damage that they might incur if they got a fall because of the negligence of the farmer. This waiver is still in existence and having consulted solicitors and barristers, I am quite convinced it is not worth the paper it is written on. I refused to implement it with the Tara Harriers but encouraged followers to take out a personal accident policy. This was a much more practical solution.

*Gustavus Villiers (Gussie) Briscoe in the
hall of Bellinter House, 1895.*

*Painting by John Ryan of the spiral
staircase at Bellinter.*

Gussie Briscoe with the Tara Harriers at Bellinter, 1895.

Cecil Briscoe with the Tara Harriers at Bellinter, 1909.

George Briscoe and Lance Smith with the Tara Harriers at Bellinter, 1950.

Freom left to right: Henry Smith, George Briscoe and Lorraine McDowell at Asigh, 1992.

Fishing party at Lough Derravaragh, 1922. From left to right: Miss Sheppard, Phyllis Briscoe, Billy Hope-Johnston, Cecil Briscoe, Sir Thomas Ainsworth, M. Delamere, Roguey Hope-Johnston and Johnnie Grant.

Hunting group at Bellinter, 1928. From left to right: Hubert Hartigan, Miss Susan Hope-Johnston, Cecil Brabazon, Miss Pean Hope-Johnston, William Fitzsimons, Cecil Briscoe, Mrs. Sue Hartigan and Aubrey Brabazon. Egidio Maccario in the background.

Cavalcade leaving Bellinter on a camping trip, 1939.

Camp at Kilnahard, Lough Sheelin, 1939.

Above: Mr. and Mrs. C. Bird, senior.

Left: Senator Quirke and Cecil Briscoe at the opening meet of the Tara Harriers at Bellinter, 1936.

A group of riding talent at the ball, 1940. From left to right: Aubrey Brabazon, Constance Briscoe, Waring Willis and Ann Chute.

The Meath Foxhounds hunt ball, 1944. From left to right: George Briscoe, Beryl Talbot, Jimmy Wilson and Stella Briscoe.

The Tara harriers hunt ball at Navan, 1948. From left to right: Louise Briscoe, George Briscoe, Constance Briscoe, Justin McCarthy, Stella Briscoe and Lance Smith.

The Marriage of George and Louise, 1947.

Cecil and Phyllis Briscoe, 1947.

8. Farming during the War, L.D.F., Air Corps

DURING the last world war, although many of my friends joined the British forces to fight against the great evils that Hitler had perpetrated, I found myself in the position that I could not do so as my father was very crippled and quite unable to cope with the running of the estate. We were obliged to till part of our land to produce enough food to keep our country going. There was rationing in England and many other countries but at the time rationing had not yet been introduced in Ireland. We did not have anything like the facilities for tilling the land that we have now. I had a couple of very good ploughmen with horses of course, who successfully tilled enough to fulfil my quota of tillage that had to be done. When the corn became ripe and ready for harvesting we got going with an old reaper and binder pulled by 3 horses.

People from towns and cities were asked to go out by the State to help save the harvest with the farmers. They were volunteers and were unpaid. I think that the State organised transport for them. So far as I can recall, they brought their own food with them. Many volunteered very cheerfully and willingly but I discovered that you had to brief them very carefully as to what you wished them to do as naturally they knew little or nothing about farming. I had my men working away as hard as they could and when they had cut and stooked a big field of corn they moved onto the next field. My town helpers arrived and as sometimes the sheaves in the stooks had to be turned to get the inside of them outside to help them to dry, I said "Go to that field and turn the sheaves in the stooks." I was away for the rest of the day and on returning found that to my amazement, that every stook in the field had been turned upside down with the head of corn on the ground. In spite of the seriousness of what had happened I could not help but laugh. They had worked so hard thinking they had done a great job.

My head ploughman, Brendan Fleming, was working a new mare I had just purchased and while putting her into the shafts of the cart she became very agitated and suddenly reared up and came down on his head and gave him a nasty gash. I brought him off to his doctor to get stitched up. Although this doctor was very able and good, he had the idea that in a case like this it was not necessary to give an anaesthetic. He sat him down and proceeded to stitch him up. I, waiting in the car, could hear screeches and shouts and did not know what was happening. He appeared shaking and said that I was never to bring him to that man again.

It was at that time that I joined the Local Defence Force (LDF) and certainly it was the nearest thing to 'Dad's Army' that you could ever find. I was appointed intelligence officer to our group. George Robinson, the famous jockey, Willie Robinson's father, was our commanding officer. A regular army officer was in charge of the whole area consisting of groups from Meath and surrounding counties. He was no other than the famous show jumper, Fred Ahearne. We would meet and parade and train about every fortnight or so. We had the River Boyne in our area and pillboxes had been installed on the south side of all the bridges over the river. It was our duty to man these in an emergency. I well remember guarding the bridge at Stackallen one night to repel the enemy. Quite who the enemy was it was not clear and I don't think we would have repelled much with a couple of old shotguns and batons.

Once when we were getting a lecture from an army man about the use of pistols, he produced an old weapon, told us all about it and in finishing up remarked, "I think this weapon would be more detrimental to the fellow firing than to the one at the other end."

A great character called Geoffrey Gilpin lived quite close to Dunshaughlin. He was in charge of a group in his area. His men appeared on parade one day. He lined them up and said, "We are going to have some parachute jumping today". They of course looked very perplexed. He marched them down to the hay barn in his yard, which had several layers of hay in it culminating in a high bank at the top. He thereupon gave each man an umbrella and marched him all up several layers of hay to the top. He then ordered, "Open parachutes!" whereupon they all opened their umbrellas. Final order "Jump!" History does not record how many casualties were suffered.

Of course we had one great advantage. Petrol was unobtainable but we as officers were given so many coupons a month, which kept us on the road. The officers met once a month and it was always a full meeting as the petrol coupons were then handed out. These were just a few of my experiences in the L.D.F.

Farmers got preference for fuel for tractors. Motorcars were very scarce. Motorists had a very small petrol allowance, so little that it wouldn't pay you to have a car. General practitioners and clerics operated under special conditions, I think. From time to time one would see terrible, black smoke belching out of car exhausts where people were trying to drive their cars on tractor fuel. Some engines must have been wrecked. Some people had gas-driven cars. That entailed putting a large tank on the roof of the car to carry the fuel. The gas, as far as I know, was generated from coal. I am not sure about the process. During the war most people had ponies and traps. Also trains were running. where the locomotives were driven by steam. I think that anything combustible was thrown into the boiler to generate the required energy. I used to use either Bective railway station or the one at Kilmessan. I used to travel to Navan or Dunboyne or Dublin and back. There were two lines from Navan. One, the Midland and Great Western, was the one I used to get to Dunboyne and onto Broadstone Station in Dublin. The other line went from Navan to Drogheda.

Bective railway station was a small, little place where you could buy your ticket and nothing more. There was no newspaper stall or anywhere to buy a cup of tea. The discontinuation of the railway line was very shortsighted, but politicians are like that. What did the State gain by selling the land along the line? Very little, I'd say. If the politicians had a little bit of foresight they could have left it there idle. Think how much it would be of use nowadays! The nature of a politician is that he or she puts himself or herself first, the party second and the State a bad third. People vote for what they get.

At that time, most of the country roads were dirt roads that had a fairly good surface. There was very little heavy traffic then, unlike now. One or two days a week I used to hack around on the roads to give the hounds some exercise. One day when I was hacking on the Bective Road at the southern end of Ardsallagh, I stopped to have a chat with a local farmer. After some pleasantries, he said to me, "What's wrong with your roof?" I said "Why? Why? I don't think that there is anything wrong." "Well,' said he, 'you'd better have a look.' From where we were standing, Bellinter House was about three thousand feet due south of us, positioned on the river terrace of the Boyne and eminently visible. I looked over and was taken aback to see that half of the back roof was gone. Well, I got a terrible shock, thanked him for having told me and said to him that I'd better see to it straight away. I galloped home with the hounds; kennelled them, and got up to see the damage. There was a huge hole where the slates were gone. I headed straight away to Kilmessan to get a team of men to fix it. There had been a bit of a storm a few nights before but I hadn't heard much or had noticed the damage at the time.

In comparison to England we were much better off because, as an agricultural country, we could supply all that we needed to eat and drink. Cigarettes, other tobacco products, and tea were rationed and in short supply. Of course there was a black market in these items so that if you were to pay the price, you could get them. Tropical fruits were unobtainable. We used to make dandelion tea by roasting dandelion roots, grating them and preparing an infusion with boiling water. It was just about potable. We also prepared dandelion salad with the leaves.

My mother was an inveterate smoker of cigarettes and it was hard to get them. Somebody told her that if she were to pick ivy leaves, dry them, crumble them and paper them up that they would produce a good smoke. The smell of the smoke was awful and it nearly killed her. Desperate people will try anything. Just imagine, smoking ivy leaves!

It was at this time during the war that the army supply column used to spend part of the summer in the Bellinter woods, under canvas, while the army were out on field manoeuvres. The army supply column had large tankers full of petrol in the woods and it really used to get to us when we would see soldiers filling hundreds of 2 gallon tins and half the time not even stopping the flow while putting the nozzle from one can to the other. Petrol flowing down the avenue! One day when driving up with my cousin, Luke Massey, he spotted a big tanker in the wood with no one around. "Drive in and we'll get a fill," says Lukie. He had the nozzle in and was just starting to pump when a soldier appeared out of the bushes and said "You'll get into trouble if you're found at that."

We had quite a few well-known people in that camp, amongst them Sir Hugh Nugent, Cyril McCormack, later Count Cyril McCormack, and Jack Stack, of show jumping fame.

As I have stated all the army and air force officers were made honorary members of Bellinter golf club and could be found there on many evenings. There was always some devilment going on and I remember one night Cyril

McCormack got quite drunk. Their camp was on the edge of the Boyne with quite a steep drop down to the river. On returning they wrapped Cyril up in a blanket and sent him rolling down the embankment. He stopped just short of the river, if he hadn't he would have got a rude awakening.

The aircraft that the air force had were very antiquated. I remember that one day when Dessie Johnson was taking off, I was out in the field with my shotgun. As he passed over, I, for fun, put my gun up and pointed at the plane. Dessie was quite perturbed and afterwards accosted me with the warning: "Don't ever do that again, you could have shot me down!" Besides Dessie there were two other officers, Kelleher and Moloney. They were great lads and full of fun.

They had a large mess tent in the woods and prior to leaving one year they gave a great party the night before going. It went on until the late hours of the morning. I well remember their chief sergeant practically on his knees praying until they all took off safely. He breathed a huge sigh of relief when they flew back over to dip their wings.

9. Marriage to Louise, Honeymoon

IN 1947 I took the most important step in my life; I married my dear Louise. We had a wonderful and enjoyable life together.

The first time that I met Louise was at a party at Jimmy Wilson's place at Boltown near Kilskyre. On reflection, that is rather ironic since after Louise's death, and after Jimmy's death, I married his widow, Jean, whom I knew at that time but not terribly well. Jimmy and Jean were not married at that time. However, after our initial meeting Louise and I became very friendly and we started to go out to dinners and parties together and became very fond of each other.

Having left school, Louise went to work as secretary to Major Gerald Tennison in his lovely old property on Lough Bawn in Co. Monaghan . She spent a busy but happy few years there and became a very dear and close friend of Ruth, the major's wife, and of all the family. Louise was working there when I first met her and it was more or less love at first sight between us. Ruth, Major Tennison's wife, was like a mother to her.

Ruth's daughter, Anne, was of the same age as Louise and became one of Louise's best friends and was one of the bridesmaids at our wedding. They were always very close and kept in touch throughout the years. Anne married and lived for some years in the Bahamas before going to live in Wales and did not see very much of each other after that.

Robin, Ruth's youngest son, was very young when Louise was at Lough Bawn but they developed a great friendship. Robin became quite famous as an explorer and wrote a number of books.

Louise's father owned a drapery business in the town of

Dundalk. Her mother had died when Louise was very young and her father married again. Her stepmother, Anne, was a delightful person. Louise had a brother, Ronnie, and a sister who was partly retarded.

Louise's aunt Emma, a sister to her mother, had a hotel at Trearddur Bay near Holyhead in North Wales. Emma was a delightful old girl and looked after Louise's sister for years and years. When she sold the hotel she bought a delightful little house right on Trearddur Bay. Upon her death, this house was passed on to Louise.

For several years when Louise had it, Lorraine, our daughter, and Jessica Willis used to go over in the summer for a month or so. In the early 1970s Louise decided to sell the place in Wales. She was absolutely robbed by whatever agent she had for she got very little money for it. If I had known then what I know now I would have advised her not to have sold it.

We got married in the Presbyterian church in Dundalk, because Louise was a Presbyterian and wished to get married in her local church. My best man was my first cousin, Aubrey Brabazon. My groomsman was George Malcolmson. Stella, my sister, was one of the bridesmaids along with Anne Tennison and Joy Stephenson. We held our wedding reception in a hotel out beyond Ballymacscanlon, at Greenore. At the time there was a very nice hotel there but it is gone now.

On the night before the wedding I stayed in the same hotel in which the reception was held the following day. Anne Tennison and Waring Willis were also staying there. We had a mock wedding in a pub in Greenore that night. Waring was up to all sorts of divilment. There was a fair amount of drink taken. Back at the hotel Aubrey got the fire hose and put it into Waring's bed. Waring got out soaked and ran into Anne's room and tried to get into bed with her but he wasn't allowed. There was a great bit of fun, anyway.

Jimmy Crothers gave over his house near Castlebellingham for a great party in the late afternoon and evening of our wedding. At that stage Louise and I had left for Dublin. However, I believe that it was a great party.

On our wedding night we stayed in a hotel in Dublin. Before retiring for the night we went out to see Aubrey's sister, Lelia, who apart from being my cousin was also a good friend of mine. She had just had a daughter at the time.

On the following morning we took a taxi to Dun Laoighre to catch the boat to Holyhead. It was a very rough crossing and poor Louise who was a bad sailor couldn't eat anything. I said to her "Don't worry we'll get you something to eat on the train on the way down to Euston Station." Of course, there was nothing to eat on the train, the *Irish Mail*; you could hardly get a lavatory on it. That night we stayed at the Euston Hotel. Next day we went to Tilbury and got the boat to Gothenburg.

We went to Sweden for our honeymoon and had a wonderful time. The boats from Tilbury to Gothenburg were like miniature liners and the food was superb. Unfortunately, the crossing was very rough and we were unable to eat as much as we would have liked.

Gothenburg is an attractive port and we spent two days there. The highlight was the trip up the Gota Canal, which goes through large lakes and over mountains across the centre of the country up to Stockholm. It took three days and two nights and was quite fantastic. Wonderful scenery and weather. Stockholm is possibly the cleanest city in the world.

Prohibition was in force while we were there. We had to eat 5 kroner worth of food to get some schnapps, which became quite expensive. Near the end of our visit we learned that there were drink coupons on our ration cards, which we had to have at the time. But when we looked for the coupons they were gone. An avaricious customs man at our point of entry must have removed them.

We were most fortunate in that we knew two young Swedish men who had worked in their embassy in Dublin. They brought us around to various eating places, on boat trips on the inner lakes, introduced us to the Irish Ambassador, and brought us to the famous bathing club on the artificial beach on the Baltic, near Stockholm.

One evening when we were walking back to our hotel having, dined in one of Stockholm's finest restaurants, I started to sing a song. Our escorts were horrified and told me to stop at once lest we should have been arrested and brought into custody.

The Irish Ambassador invited us to a dinner at his residence one evening. On our arrival, we were greeted warmly and were told that, in our honour that the meal was to be bacon and cabbage.

Sailing one day on a pleasure boat on the inner lakes, I sang a song. The Swedes are rather reserved but their reaction to my singing was amazing. From everywhere, cups of tea and food appeared but no alcohol of course, because of prohibition.

The day that we went to the bathing club was most illuminating. The changing rooms were arranged in an arc around the artificial beach. The women's changing rooms were arranged to one side with the men's on the other. To our amazement, everyone was naked. No fraternising was allowed on the shore but all could do what they liked in the water.

Another day we went to the races at a nearby racecourse. We went with someone whom we had met and who was supposed to have been very knowledgeable about the form. Our wagering was very unsuccessful until I noticed a horse called *"Irish Boy"* in an an up-coming race. "Oh, he is no use", our friend said. Just for fun I put a few kroners on him and he won at about twenty-five to one ! It just shows that no knowledge can come right.

10. Return to Bellinter, Farming

W E RETURNED to Bellinter to a wonderful welcome from our relatives, workforce and friends.
Louise got into the swing of things in Bellinter very quickly. She hunted regularly with the Taras and took over the whipping-in and became field master.

When we took over Bellinter we decided that we would run our hunt ball there, my parents having left to take up residence in a small house that they had built for themselves at Bellinter Bridge. Although we had previously run a couple of hunt balls for the Meath Hunt at Bellinter House, it later became a fairly regular function for the Taras. There were wonderful parties that usually went on until breakfast time. We threw open the whole house. Dancing took place in two drawing rooms. Mrs. Lawlor of Naas did the catering. It seems quite incredible that we could have 400 guests in the house and give each of them a sit-down supper and have all-night dancing, for the princely sum of two pounds per head!

It was of course a great challenge to Louise coming in to live and work in such a large and uneconomic place like Bellinter. However, We were both young and enthusiastic, and although it was hard work, we loved the place and we were very happy there. We worked hard and sported likewise. We kept dry stock and cultivated a limited amount of land in growing mangolds and turnips in order to provide feeding for our cattle and sheep. At that time all the tillage had to be done by horsepower: the ploughing, tilling, sowing and harvesting. I had two very good workhorses and it is quite amazing upon looking back to see how much we accomplished with them. I had an excellent ploughman, three or four farm workers and a herd. I recall that I often grew six or seven acres of potatoes. That entailed ploughing, harrowing, raising drills with a double plough, spreading dung on the drills, dropping the potatoes and earthing them with a double plough. What an operation!

We also had a considerable acreage under meadow. Here again, we had to mow with horse-drawn machines, turn the hay with a swathe-turner, collect the hay with a hay rake, gather the hay with a hay tumbler and have a team of men to build hay cocks in the fields. That was all a big job but worse when one had eighteen acres of hay on the ground ready to be cocked with the weather looking ominously bad. However, having done all that work we were still not finished. Giving the cocks of hay a few days to settle, we then had to go around pulling hay from the butts and putting it on the head, after that we raked the cocks down and secured them with ropes. They were fairly waterproof at that stage and could be left out for a while. The last procedure was to winch a cock at a time up on a hay bogey and bring it to the barn where we made large ricks with them from which we fed the animals during the wintertime. There was virtually no silage then and, of course, no hay balers.

We also grew a certain amount of oats, principally for our hunters, but also for our occasional racehorse. This again involved ploughing, harrowing and sowing. Reaping was undertaken by a reap-and binder-machine that was drawn by three horses. The sheaves that the machine produced were put into stooks in the field to dry out. After that the sheaves were made into pikes or stacks and later drawn to the farmyard to be threshed. Threshing was usually done by a contractor with a threshing machine that travelled around doing this job for the farmers. I should point out here that a pike was a round stack of hay or corn whereas a rick was a long stack that would be made for a greater quantity of crop.

Threshing of the corn was a big operation in the farming world in those days. At the farmyard the threshing machine would turn up usually drawn by a steam engine but sometimes by one of the early type of paraffin-driven tractor. To keep the operation going along smoothly required between twelve and fifteen men. Neighbouring farmers and their men came in to help. A big lunch' of bacon, cabbage and potatoes was laid on, and, of course, a liberal supply of Guinness's stout. It was a great social occasion and an event for great camaraderie.

Economically, dry stock was not leaving much reward for all the work that we put into the operation. My great friends, the Craigie family, who at that time ran *Merville Dairies*, and were the largest suppliers of milk in the Dublin area, suggested to me that I should get into the dairy business. In 1949 I decided upon this so off I went on the trail of buying forty or fifty cows. There were fine old cattle yards at Bellinter at the time so that it was not a great job to fix up a fine long shed for the cows and to provide a milking parlour.

Having purchased the requisite number of cows, the operation got under way. I hired an excellent cowman and things went really well. Every morning a *Merville Dairies* lorry collected our milk produce. It was hard work but rewarding, which made it all worthwhile. Louise helped greatly in keeping records of each cow's production, dates of calving and such like. We decided to retain all our calves as I had a large amount of land and buildings in which to accommodate them.

During these years I continued hunting the Tara Harriers in which activity I was most ably supported by Louise, who was a most efficient and excellent Field Master and Secretary, the latter, is a position, which she held for over fifty years. At that time we also hunted with the Meath Hounds. How we found time to hunt with both packs considering all the farm work that we had on hand surprises me when I think of it.

11. The Butler

EGIDIO MACCARRIO, our marvellous Italian butler, influenced me greatly in my early life. He had come to my grandfather at Bellinter in 1903. He was a most lovable character and was immensely popular with all the neighbours. They would contact him for almost anything. In fact, they would call him in before a doctor was called. He arranged wakes and weddings; he would take on anything.

Maccarrio had quite a colourful life. His family in Italy were royalists at the beginning of the twentieth century. During the troubles there his father was killed on the doorstep in front of him. Maccarrio was stabbed in the head but survived the assassination attempt and, although very young at the time, he fled the country and arrived in the North of Ireland. He had spent a little while there before coming to my grandfather at Bellinter.

When the First World War broke out, Maccarrio enlisted with a northern Italian regiment. Throughout the war there was no word from Maccarrio. When the war ended in 1918 there was still no word from him so my parents presumed that he had been killed. At some time in 1919, to the amazement of my parents, he walked into the house and said to my father: "I could not leave you, master". It later transpired that he had a distinguished war record, having been captured twice and escaped twice from captivity.

In 1952 a telegram in Italian arrived and all I could understand was a word that sounded like 'deceased'. Maccarrio came along, read it and said, "I am the last". The telegram had notified him of the death of his sister who had married a man of great standing and fortune. At one time she had been a lady-in-waiting to the Queen of Spain.

He was left a large amount of money and a very large mansion in Turin. He left us to claim his inheritance. Both

Louise and I were very sad seeing him off as we felt that we would never see him again for at that time he was over seventy years of age.

I received letters from him saying that he did not like it there and that all his so-called friends only wanted his money but that none of them would get it as he was going to leave it to me. However, he died without having left a will. We were led to understand that along with the house he also inherited a large cellar of wine. It appears that this got the better of him. When in Ireland he had been used to drinking Guinness and whiskey. Later on I received a letter from his solicitor saying that there were so many claimants on his estate that he did not believe that anyone would get much in the end.

When we had hunt balls in Bellinter it was the practice at that time that two gardai from the local barracks were sent out to Bellinter to see that the function was properly run and that the licensing laws were observed. We had a licence for the bar up to 1 o'clock in the morning, but since the dance would continue until 7 or 8 o'clock in the morning, it did not suit the festivities to have the bar shut down at 1 o'clock. When the gardai arrived, my father said to Maccarrio "Look after those two guards." After a few hours, my father seeing Maccarrio said "Are those two guards all right?" "Oh, yes, master, one is down in my pantry and the other is in bed with the servant girl." One of the guards was a teetotaller but that did not deter Maccarrio in keeping them both out of the way and keeping the bar open.

He had been so long in Bellinter that many of the locals believed that he would come back to haunt them. I remember one night when my brother-in-law, Lance Smith, was going to bed in Bellinter. As he walked up the large front stairs, a large picture of King William at the Boyne came crashing down at his feet, an event commonly associated with a death. It is uncanny that this occurred at the time that Maccarrio had died in Italy.

There was also another amusing instance, which is worth recording. Louise had a lunch' party for two very important people, Major Tennison and Commander Adair. Unfortunately, the serving girl, whom we had, became ill just before their arrival. In desperation, we dressed up our old charwoman, who was seventy-five years of age, to do the serving. We had a very good cook who had worked for many years at Bellinter, a great deal of the time with Maccarrio. We had our starter, which worked out all right. We waited and waited but there was no sign of the next course. After some time I went out to see what was happening, and to my amazement, found the cook and the old girl on their knees praying beside the lift which brought the food up from the kitchen to the next floor. "What on earth has happened," I said. In unison they wailed, "Maccarrio has taken the dinner, I know it, I know it!" I put my hand on the rope for raising the lift and gave it a good pull and there was our lunch', stone cold by then. What had happened was very simple. They had put the lunch' in the bottom compartment of the lift in the kitchen and had only brought it up level with the top compartment at the next floor!

Maccarrio was a very distinguished-looking man. I remember one time he went down to help my aunt, Mrs. Cecil Brabazon at a Naas Harriers hunt ball. During the night Lukie Massy said to the photographer that it was extraordinary that he was taking pictures of everyone but not one of the most important man in the room. "Who is that?" enquired the photographer. "The Italian ambassador," replied Lukie, "And there he is over there." He was photographed at all angles. We got some excellent shots and a good laugh. Later that night or the following morning at Cecil Brabazon's, Maccarrio was carrying a tray of glasses and fell down four steps. "Are you dead?" shouted my aunt. "I will tell you that in the morning, mam," was his reply.

It was on the night of this hunt ball that a German bomber jettisoned his bombs on the Curragh. Going home to stay at Rangers' Lodge with Cecil and Gladys, I was being been driven by Luke Massey. There was quite a lot of snow on the ground and as we came to the Curragh some soldiers appeared shouting, "Take cover, we are being bombed." Where we were meant to take cover out on the plain we did not know. In the confusion, we got off the road and got lost on the Curragh and could not find our way back to a road. We then saw an explosion in front of us. That certainly sobered us up. Eventually, we found a road and got back to base in a form of disarray. One of the bombs had fallen beside Bob Griffin's house, next to the Curragh racecourse, and had not exploded!

12. Sale of Bellinter, the Bird Family, Trip to the U.S.A.

A T AROUND the beginning of the nineteen fifties I was finding it financially very difficult to keep up Bellinter. Even with a lot of support from Louise, dairy farming was just keeping the wolf from the door. I did not think that Louise and I could continue to do all the hard work indefinitely as we were getting older. Both to my bank manager and to me it was evident that things were not going well and were unlikely to improve. At the time we did not have a family but if we had we would have been fearful of leaving such a lovely and large but uneconomic place to the succeeding generation.

In 1953 I reluctantly decided that I would put Bellinter on the market. The property had been entailed in 1899 whereby Bellinter Estate was settled on G.V. Briscoe for life and thereafter to the use of his first and other sons in tail male. The property was disentailed in 1942 and in 1944 my father conveyed his life interest to me so that I was free to dispose of it. Thoughts of selling the place upset me greatly at the time, but with rising labour costs and the expense of the general upkeep of a very large place to contend with, it appeared the only sensible solution. I was not in debt to the bank at that time but it seemed that that situation would not last too long if I attempted to carry on. We had a few would-be buyers but nothing concrete until 1954. In the meantime there seemed to be a very good prospect for tillage so I started to plough up a good part of the farm.

A Yorkshire man called Bill Holdsworth appeared on the scene and, after considerable haggling; a price of 36,000 pounds was agreed. There were almost 800 acres in the property of which 250 acres were woodland and 60 acres used as a golf course. In these days, 50 years later, it sounds a ridiculously low price but it does give a very good idea of how the value of money has shrunk since that period. However, that ended a most happy and wonderful time in my old home, Bellinter, with my dear and wonderful wife, my darling, lovely Louise.

Holdsworth did not really want the house but only the land at the time. A good few years later his plans changed and he, his lovely Dutch wife, Didian, and their family came to live there.

When I sold out to Holdsworth, I wanted to retain the golf club but Holdsworth would not agree. I was fearful that he might close the place down and I was anxious to keep it going. My income from the place was sixty pounds per year, that is an annual rent of one pound per acre. Not a lot of money! However, I would have liked to have held onto it. In 1963 Holdsworth sold out to the Land Commission. Presumably, the golf club, in which I was not involved as a playing member at the time, found it easy enough to deal with the Land Commission because they bought the land and also Cluide Wood. Cluide Wood stretched for about three thousand feet along the south side of the Skane River and was about one thousand feet wide. It was a very fine wood of mixed broad-leaved trees. Sometime afterwards the wood was felled, leaving the club with enough land to extend the course to eighteen holes. After this, membership began to grow so that the club decided to build a new clubhouse. The old clubhouse was demolished and was replaced by a modern, fine building. In recent times the club acquired more land and built a further nine-hole course, so that now the club has twenty-seven holes. In the 1990s a very grand, new clubhouse was built which cost a lot of money to construct. I was at the opening being an honorary life member. Before me, my mother was an honorary member and, in his time, my father was club president.

In my playing days I could hit the ball a long way but it usually went in every direction except straight. However, occasionally it did do that for a couple of rounds and when this happened, I played quite well and subsequently I had my handicap shortened by a few strokes. I did succeed in getting down to a nine-stroke handicap but I very seldom could play to that.

Being very busy running the estate I had little time to play much golf and gave it up in 1951. The memories I have most of golf is that when we had to ride our bicycles to play during the war, there being very few cars on the road at the time. We would finish up as usual at the nineteenth hole. Having had an amount of liquor it was quite a job to mount and ride our bicycles in the dark. There is quite a steep hill on the way down from the golf course towards Bellinter crossroads. One night as I was cycling down the hill I heard an unmerciful crash behind me. My first thoughts were that somebody had been killed because of the dreadful clatter. I stopped, and in the near dark managed to recover a figure and his bent bicycle from the side of the road. It was my bank manager who, fortunately, had suffered no serious harm. However, he was unable to remount his bicycle and finally threw it in the ditch and walked back the 5 miles to Navan. It was only in daylight, having sent his porter out to collect it, that he discovered that the handlebars were out of line with the front wheel because of the crash. He lined up his handlebars, tried to mount but in the dark he could not see that his front wheel was pointing towards the ditch. No wonder that he went into the ditch every time he attempted to mount! So much for my brief encounter with golf!

In 1963 Holdsworth sold out to the Land Commission and Bellinter lands were settled by families from the west of Ireland. Each family got, I think sixty or seventy acres upon giving up their holding from where they came. A small cottage was built upon each farm for the new owners. This policy of settling westerners in the east was not well conceived because the holdings were uneconomic. This became apparent as time went on. At present, most of these farms are run on a part-time basis. No doubt some were very industrious and successful and increased their holding to a large extent by buying out their neighbours. That is how things go.

Sometime around the late sixties an order of nuns bought Bellinter House and about ten acres of land from the Land Commission. This order was known as the Sisters of Sion, an order that had been founded in order to promote understanding between Christians and those of the Jewish faith. The nuns organised and ran seminars on different religious topics. I knew some of them very well and thought that they were great people. In fact, they gave me permission to have a few parties at Bellinter House when they occupied it. I heard someone once say that George Briscoe was the only man that he knew that, having sold his house about fifty years ago, was still hosting parties in it! Sadly, in 2004 the nuns sold out to a group of businessmen who plan to turn the place into a hotel.

My plan was to look around for a smaller place and to continue farming. Fate intervened however, and changed our whole lives dramatically.

Mr. and Mrs. Charles Bird from Boston, Massachusetts had owned Bective House since 1923. Bective House is the nearest large house to Bellinter.

The circumstances whereby Mr. Bird senior purchased Bective are interesting. On occasions in the early 1900s Mr. Bird used to come to Ireland to hunt. When doing so in Co. Meath he stayed at the Club House Hotel in Navan, which at that time was run by James Mullen. While hunting with the Meath Hounds one day near Bective his horse ran away on the road and he found himself going up a long avenue that led to Bective House. Some years after this, during the Civil war, the property came up for sale. The Stern family who were Welsh owned the place at that time. They became apprehensive about the political situation in Ireland and decided to return to Britain. They had spent a lot of money on the property and it was in top class condition. On hearing about this, James Mullen got in touch with Mr. Bird in the U.S. and said, "Why don't you buy this?"

Mr. Bird used to travel up to Boston by train and on one such occasion tossed James Mullen's letter over to two of his friends, Mr. Macomber and Mr. Tucherman and said, "Do you want to buy a fine property in Ireland?" They all had a good laugh about it and for fun decided to put in a bid of 3,000 pounds for the place. They promptly forgot all about it until one day Mr. Bird received a wire saying, "Congratulations, you own Bective." They were of course quite amazed. Mr. Bird decided that he had better get over to Ireland and do something about it. That was in 1923. On his arrival he camped in the house with no furniture and set about getting staff, furniture and all the immediate requirements. He advertised for a domestic and in due course a lovely girl appeared in the teeming rain. She had cycled her bike from Slane in order to apply for the job. Mr. Bird immediately gave it to her. Her name was Christine Fleming and she stayed with the Birds as housekeeper for forty years. She was a most attractive, efficient and wonderful girl and became an institution at Bective.

Recruiting the outside staff was the next problem. Mr. Bird knew an attractive Irishman who had gone to live in Boston and who drove a taxi there. He got in touch with him and gave him the job as agent in Bective to run the farm and the place. He was Tom Lavin, the father of our famous short story writer, Mary Lavin. Tom Lavin was a most colourful character and was very well known locally and in the horseracing world in Ireland. Things went ahead and an excellent staff was got together and Bective was kept immaculately.

Mr. Macomber embarked on a liner to come and visit the property in which he a third share. The liner docked at Cork where he had planned to disembark. He had two of his dogs on board but he was not allowed to bring them into Ireland unless they were quarantined. He refused to allow this, stayed on the liner and never came back to visit Bective. Sometime later he sold his share in the property to Mr. Bird.

Mr. Tucherman came over off and on for some years until he, too, eventually sold his share to Mr. Bird.

Upon the death of her father, Tom Lavin, Mary Lavin, and her husband, William Walsh, took over the management of Bective. Tragically, William died at a very young age. As Mary did not wish to continue managing the place on her own, Mr. Bird was on the look out for a replacement.

The Birds' son Charlie junior, was a friend of mine and he got in touch with me and asked me if I would look after Bective until his father could get to make some arrangements. I agreed to do so.

A couple of months later Mr. Bird senior arrived over. He and his wife, Julia were really fine people whom I had known for some years. He asked me what I had planned to do when I left Bellinter and I told him that I was looking around for another place. "Why don't you come over to Bective, live in the wing and look after the place?" he asked. "That sounds very good to me", I replied. However I told him that there were certain problems that I would have to solve before I could move. "What are those?" he asked. I told him that I wished to carry on hunting the Tara Harriers and would have to find kennels for the hounds and stabling for my four or five hunters. "That is no problem", he said. "Bring them all over with you".

It so happened that a former master of the Meath Hounds, John Watson, had owned Bective at the beginning of the century and had kept his hounds there. The disused kennels were still there and were able to be fixed up at not too great a cost. There was also a fine horse yard with over twenty stables. It was all agreed there and then and so started the most wonderful life and relationship with the Bird family that, thank God, lasts to the present time.

We decided that we would have an auction of most of the house contents at Bellinter in the springtime. When we told Charlie Junior and his wife about our plan, they invited us to the States that summer. We stayed in their beautiful home at Ipswich, Massachusetts and had a truly great time.

Our trip to the States was wonderful. On our arrival at Sunswick, Ipswich, we found Charlie madly driving around the countryside in his pick-up van in an attempt to find and capture his Hereford bullocks that had broken out from his farm. There is a vast area of woodland and unfenced land there and it was an almost impossible job to find the wandering cattle and then to round them up. Charlie's telephone was constantly ringing with information on sightings and complaints about destruction to peoples' gardens. Four of the bullocks had been killed in traffic accidents on the highway. Desperate as Charlie might have been, his good friend and insurance broker, Herbie Tuckerman, who had insured them, was going almost crazy. In the end, some were captured and some were destroyed. History does not relate how much this mishap cost the insurance company.

Charlie had some corn that badly needed to be weeded with a tractor-drawn grubber. However, he didn't have time to do it while the search for his cattle went on. I volunteered to do it for him, so on my second day in the States I was out in the open country doing what I had done many times at home in Ireland. It was a very warm and humid day and I was bent over all the time doing the work. That evening I felt rather queer. Charlie and Neenie, Charlie's wife, said that I would be all right and to have a drink.

The hospitality was unbelievable. On almost every night there was a party. I complained that I did not feel so good but got little sympathy. "Only a hang-over," they said. After about six weeks I said to Neenie that I had better go and see their local G.P. The doctor took a good look at me and told me that I presented a very severe case of sunstroke. He told me to go home and to stay in bed for a few days and that on no account was I to take a drink, as it could be the death of me. "Doctor," I replied, "If that is the case I should have been dead weeks ago."

Although I had not played golf for a few years before I went on holiday to the United States, I let slip that I had played for a time to a moderate standard in Ireland. The consequence of such an admission was that I was roped in to play in a couple of their tournaments at Myopia and at Essex.

I played with Corgie Cheston at Myopia. He was a scratch player so patently very good. We were the favourites the night before to win at the auction sweep. Denny Boardman appeared at the tee at tee-off time but there was no sign of his partner. Corgie kept saying "Poor, Denny, too bad." We started away and Corgie could not hit a thing. I played well for me but Denny knocked the devil out of us both. That was the end of our aspirations in that event.

In the Essex tournament, I was to partner Harry Dreaper, otherwise known as *Harry the Horse*. I thought that I was to suffer the same fate as Denny had undergone in the previous competition, as there was no sign of Harry. We were playing the favourites from New York, one of the two was a scratch player and the other had a handicap of plus one. I suffered stage fright in taking those two on. A short distance down the fairway in front of the first tee there was a brook into which one's ball was bound to go were one to strike it along the ground. I took a swipe with my iron and topped the ball and along the ground it went. However, I was lucky because my ball happened to bounce along and over a nine-inch wide plank, which was used as a bridge by the players to cross the stream. My second shot was similar to the first in outcome in that once more I hit the ball a short distance and along it bounced over the ground again. By this stage Harry had arrived, half-dressed and hit off the tee after us. I hit a magnificent shot for my third to the corner of the green. Our opponents were not bothering too much with me and were more interested in Harry's progress. When we were all on the green they asked Harry how many shots he had taken. As my ball was farthest from the pin I was the first to putt and holed for a four right across the green. "Oh, how many is that?" one of them asked casually. "A four, net three with a stroke," said I. They were amazed and rattled and we took them to the eighteenth hole before they succeeded in beating us. After that, they went on to win the competition. Following that I played no more golf on my visit.

Charlie, Louise and I flew down to Albany to go to the Saratoga sales and races, which we enjoyed greatly. At that time there was a strike in all the large, inland airlines so we flew with a practically unknown airline, called Mohawk Airlines, in a DC3. On our return, one engine refused to start and Louise was getting quite nervous and agitated about this. Charlie was reading a book and said, "What are you worried about, we are still on the ground, ain't we?" Eventually we got going and, in spite of having to fly around two electrical storms, we made it back safely to Boston.

We spent a very enjoyable weekend up in York Harbour, Maine. We had lots of lovely food and good drink. When I am in my cups with my pals I am wont to get up and sing an odd song or two. Up there I was taken aback to find that every time I stood up with the intention of singing, there were loud shouts of "Sit down!" I thought this pretty rude to say the least. It was later that I was told that there was a law in Maine, which prohibited the consumption of alcohol in a public place while standing.

We had a lovely week staying with Mr. and Mrs. Bird Senior in their holiday house at Chappaquiddic, Martha's Vineyard. The beaches there are magnificent and the town of Edgarton is most attractive. At the southern end of Martha's Vineyard there was an Indian settlement that was most interesting. Also at Martha's Vineyard there were thousands of lobsters and crayfish in large tanks where one could have a good look at them.

The house where we stayed was beside the bridge where Ted Kennedy later went into the drink with Mary Jo Kopechne. I used to go down to a small harbour to fish there.

As things occur, our time came to end this wonderful holiday. We had to return to Ireland to get down to moving house and down to work

13. Move to Bective House

ON OUR RETURN home from the United States we had the daunting task of having to move house from Bellinter to the wing at Bective House. This was quite an operation as there was an accumulation of property and effects from several generations. However, we were lucky in that there was a great deal of space at Bective so that we were able to store whatever we did not ordinarily require or were unable to fit into the wing.

When we had completed the move there was no respite. Apart from taking over the running of the estate, I had to set about buying twelve to fifteen hunters for Charlie, who at that time, had taken upon himself the joint mastership of the Meath Hunt. Charlie Cameron and I purchased a really top class stable of hunters. Quite surprisingly, we did not lay out big money for any of them.

One day a lorry load of drink of all descriptions turned up. I was amazed, I had never seen such an amount of alcohol delivered to a private house before. Suffice to say in spite of many parties and a constant stream of visitors that lorry load of drink lasted for the five years of Charlie's joint mastership. Charlie Cameron came to live in Bective and we all lived in the wing. There were constant games of poker and bridge. Neenie was practically obsessed with hunting and hunted as much as she possibly could. She and I made quite a few forays to hunt with neighbouring packs. The sport was good with the Meaths and the Taras and the parties and fun were wonderful.

The next step was to procure a good headman and other staff to look after them. We were particularly lucky in this regard in that I hired George Bell as headman. He had worked for several years as head man with Ginger Wellesley, who trained horses at Kildalkey. Previous to that he had been stud groom for twenty-five years with Lord Fingal. He was an excellent man with horses and also a good judge of cattle. He remained with us until his death in the 1980s.

Lord Fingal told me an amusing story about George Bell who had a reputation as a woman fancier. One day George and the local vet, Lewis Doyle, were treating a foal when the animal kicked George in his family prospects. George was hopping around in great pain and distress shouting, "Oh, my private parts, oh, my private parts!" Lewis Doyle interjected: "Private parts be damned, you've been hawking them around for years."

Between the hunt horses and those of Neenie Bird, those of Louise and mine, we kept approximately twenty animals, which necessitated having five to six staff to care for them during the winter. Late summer was a very busy time at Bective in getting the horses and hounds fit and generally making all the preparations for the hunting season.

Since there were three packs of hounds hunting a considerable amount of the same farmland, it was quite a job to fit the meets in to the calendar so that no two packs would hunt over the same area within a reasonable time. There was never a great problem in fitting in the Meath Hunt and the Tara Harriers meets but the Ward Union Staghounds were a different proposition because they sometimes ran great distances and would not know where they might end up. George Malcolmson, my first cousin, was the master of the Wards at the time so, in order to sort out the fixture and location list, so to speak, Charlie Bird, Charlie Cameron and myself used to meet up with him each month in the season. Over a few drinks and with friendly acrimony, we sorted out our cards, and everything worked pretty well.

Nowadays it is not so easy for the foxhounds and the harriers to fit in with the staghounds. This situation has been brought about because of modern farming practices and because there are more livestock in the fields at present and there are more stud farms also. There is also the difficulty of giving farmers, over whose land the hunt takes place, adequate notice. The harriers and foxhounds provide the farmers with ample prior notice of the intent to hunt, especially in confined areas. The staghound hunters persist in saying that they cannot give notice because they do not know where the hunt is going to take them. This may be so but I maintain that if they were seen to make an effort of 'warning' say, within a five-mile radius of the meet, it would bring them a considerable amount of goodwill.

However, I digress. A very fine *Lambourne* horsebox was purchased and so the set-up for several epic years was complete.

At this time, I hunted the Tara Harriers in the Navan-Kells area, and Joe Moorehead hunted the Trim-Enfield. Our kennel huntsman was Christy Dowdall. We had a nice pack of hounds, showed good sport and we were well supported.

14. Lorraine

SOMETIME after Louise and I had been going out together and when we were becoming serious about each other, she was very honest and straight with me and told me that when she was fourteen years of age that she had to have a hysterectomy operation with the result that she could not have any children. I said that that was too bad but as we loved each other that it didn't matter. My father, although he was far from being anti-Louise, was disappointed that I wasn't going to have children. We decided that we were getting married anyway and that that was the end of it. I have never regretted it. We had fifty-four years of a very happy marriage.

Louise had always said that she would love to adopt a child or two. The wife of the doctor who had carried out the operation on Louise was a member of the Protestant Adoption Society of Ireland and a very lovely person. We were in constant touch with the society for several years. One day she contacted Louise and told her that she had found someone suitable for us. She told us that there was a female child that was of the same background as ourselves and that our application to adopt her would be successful. That was 1956. We were delighted. Does it matter how children come? Of course not! We loved Lorraine as a natural child and I continue to do so. We were terribly lucky.

We were living in Bective at the time. Charlie Bird had always been very good to her and has been very fond of her.

After our move to Asigh Lorraine started school. She first went to the little Church of Ireland school at Trim where she was lucky in that three of her best pals at the time also attended. They were Jessica Willis, Susan Evans, Lelgarde's daughter, and Bill Holdsworth's daughter. Before going on to secondary school, Lorraine attended Hill Court School for about two or three years.

When Lorraine left Hill Court some of her best pals told her that they were going on to St. Columba's School in Rathfarnham. Lorraine was mad to go there. That was the first year that St. Columba's was taking in girls. Before that it had been a boys' school. However, Louise said that she had to go to Alexandra College on Earlsfort Terrace. Louise had gone to school there. Lorraine didn't like that idea at all but started at Alexandra. When the school moved out of the city centre to the outer suburbs, Lorraine hated it. I had to agree with Lorraine. It was like a bloody jail. You'd go to bring her out and you couldn't get in. You had to ring bells and wait around in frustration for somebody to come out to let you in. I hated the place too. Louise softened on my prodding and after only one term Lorraine moved to St. Columba's.

She had a great time at St. Columba's. I remember one time that we got a school report from the school mistress which said that she was not doing any work there and so on. We got awfully worried. However, when the exams came up, she headed the class, she beat them all! I think that the schoolmistress must have been flabbergasted with that. Oh, she has a good brain.

When she left St. Columba's, Lorraine went to work with the Irish Nationwide Building Society in Dublin. At that time she shared a flat with a few pals in Ballsbridge. She worked there for a few years until she landed a job with the Dairy Board, An Bord Bainne.

Bob Lucas-Clements who was a great friend of ours and who also hunted with us had become head of the Dairy Board around that time. Before that he ran a glassware company, Cavan Crystal. He was looking for someone to deal with French clients as the Board did a lot of business in France. As Lorraine was a very good speaker of French and had been over to France on several occasions, Bob took her on. She was essential to him, Bob said because Lorraine could natter to the French people whereas Bob didn't have a clue.

When Lorraine got married to John McDowell, who had been at St, Columba's with her, Bob was all upset. He said to her, "When you get married can you spend a few days a week up here?" Lorraine enjoyed working at the Dairy Board very much but, upon her marriage, she intended to settle down and to create a home with John and to live in the country again. She found it impossible to accept Bob's offer even though she liked him and the whole set-up at the Dairy Board.

15. Work at Bective, Hunting

HAVING moved our hounds to their new kennels and ourselves to the wing in Bective House, the big decision to be made was how to continue running the place. The house which was a fine property, was built by Bolton in the 1800s. This is the same man that built Bective church and also the Catholic church at Robinstown. Bolton did a lot of tree planting and laid out beautiful walks through the woods. He also established a lovely walled garden from which we used to sell produce in our time there. When we were there the place was very well kept with a fair number of staff and obviously the upkeep of the place cost a lot of money. The main object was to keep expenses down as much as possible because what money that could be made from stock at the time was very little. Mr. and Mrs. Bird Senior were great people and we had a very good and happy relationship.

Firstly I set about improving the land and making out a plan to carry as much stock as we could with a view to alleviating the cost of running such a large and uneconomic place. We were fortunate in that we had an excellent staff in our employ. Jim Clarke was the handy man who looked after the hunt clothes and all repairs. Paddy Flanagan was the tractor man. As strong as an ox, he got through everything, including the machinery. We had a saying: *Paddy break all and Jim mend all.*

The garden was very attractive and extremely well kept by Tom Hopkins. Apart from gardening, one of the jobs assigned to him was looking after the water pump on the River Boyne. What a job! We were forever in trouble with the pump breaking down and the place without water. Regarding water, I am reminded of the hot water system, which very often did not function. Neenie Bird would come down the corridor shouting, "Manager, no hot water, again!"

This problem went on sporadically for a considerable time. One day I walked into a bathroom and discovered Charlie Cameron fast asleep in the bath, with the hot water tap fully open and his toe stuck in the tap. I found Neenie and told her that it was not any wonder that there was no hot water when her boyfriend baths with the hot tap open and hot water pouring out through the overflow.

Another permanent member of the staff was Kevin Costello. Kevin was a most delightful old man who had spent most of his life working at Bective. He kept all the paths, avenues and lawn surrounds always looking immaculate. It was only when he and we left Bective that I really appreciated what a wonderful job he did.

The work that necessitated all the horses being kept very well and efficiently and the foxhounds to be looked after required a large staff in the yard. In days gone by it had been the practice of the master of the hounds and his hunt to have second horses for hunting days, a practice strictly adhered to by Charlie Bird. On dropping three horses at the meet, the horsebox returned home for three more, met at a pre-arranged place, changed horses, returned with the three horses that had hunted, and returned at the end of the hunt to collect the other, spare three horses and bring them back home. Horses hardly ever got hurt and there is no doubt in my mind that it was because of substitution. If horses did suffer any injury, it happened when they were tired, but not with us! What a stable of horses we had! They were brilliant! I bought the hunters at various places around the country, and as I have mentioned, paid no big price for any of them. Much credit of course must go to our wonderful head groom, George Bell.

Hunting went on apace with both packs. Sport was up and down, but generally good, and always fun to be out in the countryside. Our relationship with farmers was excellent. When I used to hunt in other parts of Ireland, I realised how tolerant Meath farmers are.

Lord Roger Mostyn was living in Meath at this time and

hunted with both packs. On one day while hunting with the Meaths at Dunderry, he got into an argument with Paddy Mulligan, a large farmer, who reared a lot of sheep. He said to Paddy that his father had many more sheep than Paddy had and that he, Mostyn, understood all about sheep. This went down very badly. On our return to Bective, Charlie Cameron was furious and sent him back to apologise to Paddy immediately.

One day, Charlie Bird, Neenie and Louise went off to hunt with the foxhounds in the Dublin end of the country. During the day, a great storm blew up. Charlie Cameron and I were at home in Bective. It got later and later and darker and darker with trees crashing down around us, one or more of which brought down the telephone line. We did not know where the three of them were and could do little except wait. Eventually, they appeared out of the darkness having had an extraordinary experience. They had spent hours driving around roads avoiding fallen trees. In the end, they were blocked. They then took their horses out of the horsebox and decided to ride home. They jumped trees on the roads, rode in and out of fields and got home in the pitch dark with the gale still howling. They sure needed a drink!

There was a most eccentric gentleman from Scotland called Jimmy Sterling-Stevenson who rented Rathaldron Castle and came to Ireland to hunt. He was very shortsighted and had to wear glasses all the time. His capacity to drink brandy was prodigious. He was going hunting at Ratoath one day and rang me to see if I would like a lift. I accepted his offer with alacrity and with thanks. He imbibed heavily during the meet and I was wondering how he would weather the day. We found and had a nice hunt over some large ditches. At the end of the hunt there was no sign of Jimmy. It transpired that he had fallen into a large ditch and had lost his glasses. Having remounted his horse with some considerable difficulty, he perceived what he had taken to be some of the hunt horses, galloped after them and was upended again in another large ditch. It transpired that what he thought were hunt horses was a herd of cattle. The ditch that he had tried to jump was quite un-jumpable. He found his way to a road and, with difficulty, back to the meet. Having been wet and blind, he cheered himself with many more brandies.

I arrived back to the meet later and loaded up my horse. Having done that, I went into the pub to find Jimmy and to have a drink. It was not long before I thought it would be mission impossible to get home with him, as he was both drunk and blind. Blind drunk indeed! He would not give me the keys to his car. Well, I have never had such an exciting and hair-raising drive in my life. Strangely enough, we made it home safely.

My next encounter with Jimmy was even more extra-ordinary. He had a Californian lady over living with him by the name of Felita Reid. She had been married and divorced a couple of times. Jimmy rang me and said, "I am going to get married and want someone to stand for me. Will you do it?" I could not refuse and told him that I would. The wedding was arranged to take place in the registry office in Kells. It was the first wedding that the registrar there had ever attempted. The wedding party arrived to find a considerable crowd from the town milling about. "What's all this?" I said. "Oh, the law states that the doors and windows of the premises have to be left open when a wedding is being conducted," said the registrar. I cannot vouch for the truth of this.

However, all being seated, the wedding proceeded. Unfortunately, the registrar had no experience whatever in dealing with sheaves of divorce papers. After numerous false starts, the registrar eventually pronounced the couple man and wife. I just have to take his word for that. Upon conclusion, about four or five bottles of whiskey appeared. Glasses were filled to the brim with neat whiskey as we toasted the newly weds. We arrived back at Rathaldon Castle where all the guests got drunk and passed out peacefully one by one.

16. Fishing

I had many wonderful days fishing at Shean Lodge on the Owenduff River, which is the property of my great friends, the Craigies. Shean Lodge is located near the village of Ballycroy in County Mayo. I particularly remember a party going down one September in the late 1950s to fish and to shoot snipe. There was Donald Craigie, George Malcomson, Lewis Doyle, Charlie Bird and Bill Holdsworth. We had a pretty hectic night and the next morning we decided to go shooting, as the river was too low for fishing and it was getting late for the salmon and sea trout anyway.

We set off for Belmullet and went into the first bog. It was pretty heavy going and Lewis decided that it was too much for him and sat down on a bank above an old boggy river. A snipe rose and Charlie shot him. He landed in very thick cover and as we had no dogs with us I said "You will never find him there". "Oh, gee", said Charlie "that is the first snipe I have ever shot so I must find him." He searched around for half an hour and nearly got submerged in the bog but never got him. Returning, we could not see Lewis on the bank and went to locate him. He had slid down the bank into the boggy river and was up to his neck in mud and water fast asleep. We extricated him and proceeded. Next we shot from a lakeshore that was covered with rushes. I shot a high snipe and it fell out in the lake. Not being used to shooting without a dog, I hated shooting a bird and not retrieving it. Shortly after that I shot another that also fell out in the lake. This was too much for me and I stripped off all my clothes and was about to dive in which fortunately I did not. I took a step in and found that it was only a couple of feet deep! The birds were out in the middle of the lake and the further I walked out the shallower it became. I retrieved my snipe, stark naked, with the water not far above my ankles. There was great amusement when an old man appeared with his horse and cart and could not make out what was going on. Not many birds were shot and we decided to make for home.

Charlie retired to bed for a rest. I went up the river and caught a small salmon. The rest of the party decided they would go in to the big hotel at Mulrany and have a few drinks. The wonderful housekeeper in Shean, Mrs. McMennaman, had a lovely dinner prepared. Charlie and I waited for a long time and had ours but still no sign of the rest, eventually we set off to look for them. Entering the hotel we heard a piano playing and great singing and jollity. They had found some young fellow to play the piano and the most hectic dancing you could imagine was in progress. "My goodness," said Charlie, "we need a few drinks before we join in that." George was not a very large man and he was having a great whirl with the manageress who was very big and strong. Every time they got really whirling well she let him go and he went crashing across the floor into something. Nothing daunted, he would pick himself up and come for more. He was fairly battered next morning.

Next morning Lewis went off to Mass. The gillie in Shean, Frank McMennaman, who had been shooting with us the previous day, could not find his gun. We searched to no avail and tried to remember what he might have done with it when we had finished up shooting on the day before. There was a wall beside a church and he remembered putting it against the wall. One of us drove him to the spot and to our amazement there was the gun still leaning against the wall. We were going out for a while after our lunch' but no sign of Lewis. We went to Ballycroy and found him fast asleep on the back pew of the church.

For many years in September my father and mother used to bring down their caravan and tents to camp on the shores of Lough Mask and to dap with daddy long legs and grasshoppers for trout. It was a lovely unpolluted lake with an abundant supply of free-rising fish and we had many memorable days. Our gillie, Johnnie Moran, was a great character. He never took an alcoholic drink in his life but was incessantly brewing up cups of tea with an old kettle and teapot. I have never seen a man with such a shake in his hand. Alcohol cannot always be the cause! My father, my uncle, Billie Leatham, and myself were out and there was nothing doing. Johnny kept saying, "Reel up and we will go to a good place." Nothing was doing so Billy said "Bring us to a bad place!" He brought us to the pike hole where one never caught anything. We proceeded to catch four or five lovely trout, to his astonishment. Thereafter, many boats were finding the bad spot with great success. On another occasion my father and uncle were out with Johnnie and I went out in another boat with Paddy, also a well-known gillie. We had good success and got a number of fish. Meeting up for lunch' the others had nothing caught. "Where did you get them?" asked Johnnie. "Here and there," said Paddy. On going home in the evening Paddy shouted to Johnnie "Did you find here or there?"

We had one very terrifying experience on Mask. We did not have our own boat down and hired one from a young lad. Unfortunately the boat was leaking quite a lot. The young fellow suddenly got up and went to go behind my father to bail the water from the boat without saying anything to anyone. He slipped and was certainly going overboard but managed to put his arms around my father's neck. Over went the boat and only that Billy, who was about 18 stone weight and myself threw ourselves on the other side and righted the boat we would all have undoubtedly drowned. When the boat came up there was only about a foot of it above the waterline with the gillie's backside over the side hanging onto my father. What an escape! There were a good few whiskeys drunk on our return. A lesson that one can never be careful enough in a boat on the lakes.

In the early 1950s while holidaying down at Roundstone with my father and mother we went over to have a drink at the hotel at Renvyle where we met Mr. Johnnie O'Rourke, a friend of my father's. He and Tom Fairhurst rented the fishery at Delphi from Lord Sligo. He asked me to come and have a days fishing but added that it had been no good for some time owing to lack of water. I was of course delighted to get a day on such a well-known river. Although I was very much a fly fisherman I asked him would he mind if I tried fishing a prawn. "We don't approve of bait fishing, but all right, try it if you wish". I had about 6 prawns and set off the next day. The gillie met me and off we went to the river and within a few minutes I hooked and landed a lovely salmon and believe it or not I had three fish on the bank by lunch' time. I had been invited by Johnnie O'Rourke to go to the lodge for lunch' and when I appeared with three salmon he was quite amazed. "We haven't' had a fish out of the river for about a month." After lunch' I enquired where I was to continue fishing. "Oh, you go out on the Finlough Lake in front of the lodge." The gillie was quite put out at leaving the river and decided we would trail a prawn behind the boat. In no time I got a strong pull. "Wind it in and see has the bait gone," says he. I had it skidding on top of the water when up came a salmon and took it, to our amazement. We landed him and the gillie asked how many prawns I had left, "Two" says I. "Oh, that's terrible," says he, "Only two more fish". We trolled it around for the rest of the day but had no more strikes. However, I always remember it as a remarkable days fishing. I heard later that Johnnie had rushed off to Leenane to try to get some prawns; that was the reason I was sent to Finlough so that he could fish the river.

We used to quite often fish Dulough, which is a lake on the Delphi fishery. It is a large deep lake lying between two mountains, which act as a funnel when the winds get up. It was famous for twisters in a strong wind and sometimes one would see columns of water going right up the mountainside. We were fishing there one day when suddenly a strong wind got up. I said that we had better get out of here quickly. We had a small "Seagull" engine on one of the large and heavy boats used on the lake. It started all right but with the waves getting bigger, one of them went over the engine and swamped it and there we were along a shore with jagged rocks all the way. I had done some rowing at school in racing fours but never did I have a tougher row to get us out of danger. We definitely had another brush with disaster. We had many great days fishing on Dulough bringing in twenty or twenty-five sea trout in a day.

Fishing one day with Archie and Pat Cooke on Glencullen Lake just above Dulough, there was very little wind with bright sunshine, which made for apparently quite useless fishing conditions. I suddenly saw a large fish slowly come to the surface, turn and go down. I had not realized for a moment that he had taken my fly but very soon discovered that this was so. It is a very clear, shallow lake and we could see the fish swimming around on the end of my line. I only had him on a light trout rod and in spite of having it well bent in him I was making very little impression. After about an hour my companions were getting restless and saying pull him up. I was loathe losing him and asked what the hurry was; the fishing conditions were useless anyway. Eventually we got him up. He was a big red fish weighing 14lbs, a large fish for there.

A rather similar experience happened to me one day on the neighbouring river, the Erriff. I was given a day's fishing there and my gillie took me to some of the best pools on the river. Conditions were not good and after fishing for a while my gillie said, "We shall go up the river and try for a sea trout." The water was very clear and there was no wind. "Put up a very light cast and we might get a trout." Fishing just below the bridge on the road to Westport I suddenly saw what looked like a monster slowly swimming up, breaking the water, and turning to go down. Fortunately I was slow to react and on lifting my rod had him hooked. Then the fun started. The gillie ran up shouting "Don't pull him too hard!" He said that because I was using a very light cast. There were lilies along the bank and he kept throwing anything he could find to keep him from swimming too near and fouling the line. After at least an hour of these antics, he succeeded in getting him on the gaff by lying half out in the water and snatching him as he swam past. A lovely fish it was that weighed about 12 lbs and an unlucky one to have been put in the bag.

I was fishing one time with Clare de Burgh and a party down at Sneem when the water was low and we were only to fish for sea trout at night. There was a large pool in front of the lodge, which was full of salmon that were waiting for water to get up the river. There were some well-known fishermen there at the time including Jim Ganly, Lord Mount Charles and George Malcomson. During the daytime there was every known bait and fly thrown at the salmon but to no avail. The head gillie told us to fish a very small fly owing mainly to the river being so low. On the second day more for fun than anything else, I put up a very large Boyne river fly, which is fished on that river for big spring fish. On the first cast a fish followed it right into the bank below my feet. I immediately whipped it off and put on an even bigger fly. With the next cast I was into a big fish and there was great excitement among the anglers. There was a large pole in the middle of the pool, which had been left there to stop poachers from netting the pool and that was an obstacle to landing the fish. After great antics running around the pool, I managed to keep him the right side of it and eventually Lord Mount Charles netted him for me.

Eels were very much desired in London and Paris and there were many eel traps on rivers all over the land. Financially, they were even more valuable than salmon traps. In my younger days I used to put out lines, baited with worms, on the River Boyne. I used always get as many as I wished for the pot. My mother used to produce stewed eel in port wine sauce, which was a great delicacy. I do not ever hear of it now.

Bobbing for eels was a very entertaining sport. We would collect a can of worms and, with a needle, thread them through hemp. When we considered that we had enough we rolled the worms into a ball. On a moonlight night we would go bobbing. This entailed putting the bundle of worms in to the river and when any contact was felt one slowly lifted the bait without shaking or jerking and one lifted an eel or two into the boat. The eels were not hooked but had embedded their teeth into the hemp on the bait ball. Provided they were lifted carefully, in they came. If one were fishing from the river bank one had to have a sheet laid out on the bank because, if the eels landed on the grass they could move quite quickly and would get lost in the dark. To kill them was a further problem. I found that the best way was to cut them at the back of their heads with a sharp knife.

Fishing at this period was also very good. Pollution was virtually unknown and the big drainage scheme on the Boyne had not at that time commenced. We would get the wonderful spring salmon on the Boyne, weighing up to twenty-five or thirty pounds. Lough Sheelin was still one of the best brown trout lakes in Ireland to where we made our usual forays and caught our share of the lovely three to six pounds trout. How sad it is to relate that, shortly afterwards, Lough Sheelin became so polluted with pig effluent that it is doubtful if it will ever return to its halcyon days.

17. Neenie

I HAD met Neenie, Charlie's wife, for the first time in 1947, the year of my wedding. She came to live at Bective for a while that year shortly after her marriage to Charlie. She loved hunting. When we went to live at Bective I got to know her pretty well. Up to the time that Charlie had become joint master of the Meath Hunt, she was over and back from the U.S. many times to Bective. However, when Charlie became joint master they moved bag and baggage to Bective.

We were all there together for seven years, living in the same house. We saw each other every day and we all played cards every night. We were living virtually as a family. Quite naturally, we all knew each other pretty well. At that time we were all great friends; there was never anything else. Neenie and I used to go off hunting and riding together. I don't think that Charlie and Neenie were all that close as husband and wife; I don't think that there was any great love between them. They lived together fairly well all right but there wasn't a great sense of affection in the situation. Neenie loved the life over here and preferred Ireland to the States. I think that she persuaded Charlie to become joint master of the Meath Hounds. When Charlie was joint master we had the life of Reilly for a good few years. Neenie loved the hunting, the parties and the whole lot.

At that time we used to have some great parties at Bective. At one of those parties, Neenie's brother, Budsie Cochrane was over from the States. He was quite a character. Budsie was a big, tough fellow and managed to get fairly well oiled. In one of the rooms there was a very large table with a central pod support upon which cutlery and plates were stacked. Budsie came in and sat on one end of the table and upended it. Budsie fell on the floor and used cutlery and dirty plates fell on top of him. It was the funniest thing! I couldn't stop laughing. There he was under a heap of cutlery and broken crockery. Neenie came in and took one look at him and was flipping mad. I remember Charlie Bird coming out and looking at the damage and at Budsie. "Thank God that it wasn't me, anyway", he said as he walked away up the stairs.

The telephone, I remember well, was right beside where the table had fallen. "Ah, gee, gimme that telephone", Budsie said. This was about one o'clock in the morning. Anyway, he started twisting the thing and awakened Dick Seery down at the exchange at Kilcarne. Dick told me afterwards that he was awakened in the middle of the night by some drunken bum up in Bective House who was looking for a telephone number in the States.

One of my friends at the time was Tom FitzHerbert. He was from Navan and was a partner in a stock broking firm in Dublin. I used to shoot a bit with him and with Ted Breslin, my bank manager. Most of the shooting that we did together was snipe shooting.

The party where Budsie upended the table was the same party where Tom Fitzherbert fell into the caviare. Tom arrived with Roonah, his wife. He had had a few scoops before he came. Neenie had prepared a huge bowl of caviare and had placed it upon a table. Tom was standing beside the table talking to somebody when suddenly he lurched and fell face down into the caviare. He came up and there was caviare all over him. Neenie saw this and said, "My God", and wasn't at all pleased.

At that time Tom FitzHerbert had been a good friend of mine. We used to see a fair bit of each other. One day we were out shooting duck and there was quite a flood on the River Boyne. Ted Breslin was on the bank of the river with his eldest son; Tom FitzHerbert was in the boat with me. After a while I said to Tom that I'd row the boat across and leave him on the bank with Ted and his son. I rowed over and there was a tree that had fallen over near the bank and the top of it was in the water. As well as that, there was a strong rush of water there. Tom had only one leg. I said to Tom, "Now be very careful, keep well up on the upper side of the boat because that rush of water could turn the boat over." I threw the anchor to Ted Breslin and there I was and Tom FitzHerbert goes and sits on the other side of the boat with the result that the boat completely turned over. We were both thrown into the water. I was bloody lucky that I wasn't drowned. I came up with boots on me and everything else. It was a miracle that Tom came up right in front of me. I grabbed him by the hair and we were swept to an island where I got a foothold. I told him not to move until I could see if I could get onto the shore. I managed to get ashore and then pulled him up. There we were on this island with Ted Breslin on the bank with the boat's anchor and the boat sunk. Ted and his son pulled and pulled but couldn't get the boat up. Tom FitzHerbert began to shiver on the island. I said that there was only one way out of the situation and that was to leap into the water and to get to the bank. That is what I did. On the bank, the three of us managed to get the boat up and we rescued Tom.

I told Ted to go to Asigh and to get a car down as quickly as possible. Tom was shivering like mad and was in danger of hypothermia. I rowed downstream to Bellinter Bridge and landed at Oak Lodge, my parents' home. The car came around quickly and Tom recovered.

In 1959 Charlie Bird gave up the Master ship of the Meath Hunt and decided that he would go back to the U.S. and start working at their large business in East Walpole. Unfortunately this started the rift in his marriage to Neenie. She loved the hunting life in Ireland and had no wish to leave.

Neenie used to hunt during that time and she knew Charlie Cameron very well. At that time Charlie Cameron was living at Curtistown, Kilmessan. Charlie was a bachelor and lived at Curtistown before he moved to Bective. He was a fair bit older than Neenie or me. When Charlie Bird took over the Meath Hounds as joint master with Charlie Cameron, the Birds invited him down to live at Bective, where he lived for several years.

Charlie Cameron started off being a huntsman for Mrs. Connell of the Meath Hunt sometime in the thirties. When the war broke out he went off to fight. After the war he went in with Mrs. Connell as joint master of the Meaths. He was joint master with her until she retired in 1954, I think. Mrs. Connell was a great woman; she kept the hunt going throughout the war years. I remember her very well.

One day before Charlie Bird had returned to the States, Charlie Cameron announced that both he and Neenie were leaving Bective. It was like a bolt from the blue to Louise and to myself and of course to Charlie Bird. We were all flabbergasted on the doorstep at Bective as they picked out a motorcar and drove away together. Charlie Bird said, "Oh, my God, Oh, my God, Vivienne is on my side, nothing will come of this". Vivienne was Neenie's mother and was a very forceful character. But sure, Vivienne couldn't do anything either. They went off to the United States and subsequently got married.

Afterwards Charlie Bird gave Neenie a divorce and gave her a very big settlement on condition that she didn't remarry. Charlie knew bloody well that she was going to marry Charlie Cameron. "So that is one bright thing I did", Charlie said.

Betty Bosley, one of the best show jumpers in the U.S., was a good friend of old Mr. Bird and came to stay for a while in Bective before the break-up. Charlie showed no affection whatever for her during her stay and it was quite a shock to Louise and to myself when we heard that they had married in the States. To my knowledge they had not gone out together when they were there. It was shortly after that when we heard that he had married her. Betty was too much horse. Betty was horse, horse, horse!

Louise and I were over in the States in 1976 and, with Charlie, we went down to see Betty at Unionville, Pennsylvania. There was a very icy reception, not so much for Louise and me as for Charlie. Things were on the rocks then. Charlie and Betty were married for fifteen years or so when they divorced.

Charlie's present wife is a lady called Sister. They had grown up together and had known each other very well. She had married twice before and her last husband died quite young. She was born Sister Sears and she and Charlie had been childhood sweethearts. We are all so happy about it and love her very much.

In the meantime, Charlie and Neenie Cameron had asked me to look out for a nice, small place for them, preferably in County Meath. I had known Colonel and Mrs. Hallowes for some years and just at that time the Colonel died. They owned a very attractive rectory at Loughcrew beside Oldcastle. I got in touch with Mrs. Hallowes and asked if she was thinking of selling and the answer was "yes". I contacted Neenie who was most enthusiastic so I got in touch with the agent and bought the place on approximately 30 acres at a very reasonable price. So started ten happy years for Charlie and Neenie at Knockbrack. They took on the mastership of the Ballymacads, which lasted until Charlie's death in 1970. Neenie carried on the mastership on her own. Inevitably she was lonely and undoubtedly I was probably her dearest friend. I was very fond of her and we saw each other as much as we could but as Knockbrack was 25 miles away and I had a lot of work in dealing with our stud farm and hunting my hounds and so on, it was not a great deal. Things carried on like this for years. However, in 1975 and very suddenly without myself and many of her best friends knowing, she married a most unattractive, big blow of an Irish-American called Joe Welsh, who had recently become a widower.

Louise and I had met Joe and Peg Welsh in Massachusetts in 1954 when out staying with Charlie Bird and Neenie. Peg was a blowsy alcoholic with a heart of gold and plenty of money. He was bombastic and with no money. They had visited Ireland a couple of times and were always saying "Oh, gee, we would like to rent a place over here." On one such visit, my mother having just died, her place, *Oak Lodge*, at Bellinter Bridge, which had been left to my two sisters, was lying vacant. Since they both had their own places they had no immediate plans for the house. I informed Peg and Joe that it might be rented and soon after that the deal was done. They lived there for two or three years in a somewhat drunken haze and then announced that they had bought some land at Johnstown, near Navan and were going to build a house. This was achieved and they lived there for a few years when Peg died. Joe was unsettled and in a short time was on the lookout for another wife. He first approached a sister of Iny Willis, a great friend of ours. She fairly quickly saw the red light and retired her interest.

Bill Holdsworth, who by this time had re-sold my old home Bellinter, passed away around this time. His lovely and most attractive Dutch wife, Didian, who we all knew very well from her time living in Bellinter, had returned to their original home in Yorkshire with her family of three sons and two daughters. Joe's next venture was to go over to Yorkshire and ask Didian to marry him. Even the thought of that appalled her and he very quickly had to think of someone else.

Before Peg died Neenie gave a party at Knockbrack to which Louise and I were invited and to stay the night. Peg and Joe Welsh were also invited but not to stay the night. All had a very good party and it then transpired that Joe and Peg were quite incapable of driving. They settled themselves down to spend the night in the drawing room but, before doing so, brought in three dogs, which they had in the car, to join them. Next morning the room was wrecked. I was appalled when I looked in. Neenie arrived on the scene and no doubt you can imagine her reaction. She never wanted to see them again.

She did relent and saw them occasionally afterwards and

of course attended Peg's funeral. Joe, on his third attempt at matrimony, approached Neenie and to my amazement and that of some of her other good friends, they were hitched up before we even knew it. Pat Herdman, a very good friend of hers, told me that he had stayed the night at Knockbrack a short time before the event and Neenie stressed her dislike of Joe to him so much that Pat was equally amazed at the outcome. However, that was it and the next time I met Neenie at Fairyhouse races she cut me dead. I heard years afterwards that Joe had ordered her not to speak to me. I never really saw or had any contact with her until Joe's death seven years later.

In the meantime they lived in Boca Raton, Fort Lauderdale in Florida for several years, a place that Neenie hated. As well as that, the fact that her brother, Budsie, Charlie Bird, Jimmy Higginson, her lawyer and very special friend, and other close friends would have nothing to do with Joe, did not help the situation. He had done his utmost to try to sell Knockbrack but fortunately she held out against him.

John and Sandra Bryce-Smith were very dear friends of Neenie and shortly before Joe's death had gone out to stay with them at Boca Raton. On their return Sandra told me that things were so bad out there that she might have to go out again. It transpired that he was desperately alcoholic, incontinent, quite impossible and refused to go into a hospital or nursing home. Neenie was looking terrible and at her wits end as to what to do about him. He got so bad however, that he had to go into hospital and shortly afterwards died.

Upon Joe's death, Neenie returned to Knockbrack, the place that she loved. I remember well the day that I first saw her upon her return to Ireland; it was at the Ballymacad Hunt point-to-point in 1983. I was very pleased indeed to see her.

I was very fond of Neenie and she was fond of me. We loved each other's company very much. We knew each other very well as we had lived in the same house at the same time for six or seven years. Our relationship had been platonic until Charlie Cameron's death. After that we became more intimate. I made it clear to Neenie that I still loved Louise dearly and that I was not going to leave her or hurt her. We used to meet in a remote bog. We were very discreet and were particular not to have been seen together in any public place. This went on for several years until her death. Although some people were suspicious about our relationship, no one could say for certain that we were having an affair. If Louise suspected anything, she never mentioned anything to me. I know that I did not cause Louise any unhappiness over it and would not have done so.

I find it very hard to express my horror when it was discovered that Neenie had inoperable and rapid cancer. She had complained for a while that she had trouble swallowing and I had persistently told her to go to a doctor and get it seen to. "Oh, this is nothing, my mother had the same problem," she said. "I shall go after our hunt ball at the end of the year." Whether anything could have been done or not if she had seen to it earlier we shall never know. There being nothing more that they could do for her in the Blackrock Clinic, she returned to her beloved Knockbrack.

John and Sandra were wonderful and looked after her until the end. I called to see her a few times but it was so distressing that I gave up and ironically Sandra told me afterwards that she did not really want me to see her the way she was. She faded away quite rapidly and died in 1988 at only 61 years of age. I often wondered if her marriage to Joe Welsh had anything to do with it since she told me after his death that the seven years she spent with him were the unhappiest of her life. My sadness was accentuated when I was asked by her brother, Budsie, to give an oration at her funeral in Loughcrew Church. I managed to do so but it was very difficult as I felt such genuine grief at saying goodbye to her.

18. Boyne Hill

IN 1959 Mr. and Mrs. Jack McNamee Sullivan and family from the United States, rented Bective House for a month from Mr. Bird. Jack Sullivan kept saying to me "Gee, I would sure love to buy a place over here". As luck would have it, Boyne Hill, a dower house, which belonged to the Gerrard family, came on the market. I said to Jack "Are you serious about wanting to buy?" "Sure," he said. "Well," I said, "I shall see what I can do but, keep away from the place because if they hear an American accent, the price will double straight away." With difficulty, I restrained him. We bought the fine old property at Boyne Hill on 120 acres in 1961 for ten thousand pounds. At that time I was fairly busy but little did I realise that I was involving myself in a lot more work. Jack insisted that I should look after the place for him. I agreed that I would keep an eye on it, but between the work at Asigh and hunting, I could not give the place much time and got little more than expenses for doing so.

At Boyne Hill a great job of work was done in renovating the house and buildings, improving the land, putting up post and rail and in bringing back the magnificent garden to its former glory.

Jack Sullivan's wife, Pauline, was an attractive person with whom I got on very well. She was from a wealthy Italian family called Gerli who at one time were the biggest importers of silk into the USA. She had great ideas for modernising Boyne Hill, which had fallen into considerable disrepair. The previous owner, Mrs. Collins, had got well into her nineties when she died and had lived there for years on her own. She had suffered a great tragedy as her only son was killed at the end of the 1939 to 1945 war.

Pauline was very good at renovation and did up all the living rooms, bedrooms and even the large basement, all in excellent taste. As in many old houses, the roof had also to be extensively repaired and central heating was installed all through the house.

They had three delightful daughters and one son, all of whom Louise and I got to know very well when they came to stay in Boyne Hill. We had many pleasant parties there and they were good times.

There was a lovely old walled garden at Boyne Hill with a stream running through it. This was completely restored. The large greenhouse was demolished and a new one built in its place. It was such a beautiful garden and we were so proud of it. Unfortunately, the people who bought the property from the Sullivans had no interest in it and the garden quite quickly went back into rack and ruin.

The contacts we had with Pauline and her family were very dear to Louise and myself. I am glad to say Johnnie, their son, is carrying on their business in New York very successfully and he owns a beautiful property in Greenwich on the outskirts of the city.

Although Jack had no previous knowledge of breeding bloodstock, he bought a number of mares. His luck was phenomenal. He bought a cast-off of the Aga Khan's called *Runaway Bride*, for five hundred guineas. Jack had the cheek to ask Captain Hall, who was manager for the Aga Khan at the time, if that price could include the cost of transport home to Boyne Hill. Jack was told to get lost. However, later in the day when the mare remained unsold, Captain Hall relented and agreed that if Jack were to buy the mare, that transport costs would be included in the price.

She was very light of bone and 'straight in front.' My cousin, Aubrey, tried to win a race with her at Dundalk but, the best he could get out of her was third place in a poor race. Jack rang me near the end of the breeding season asking my advice on a top nomination for her. All the top sires would have been booked up by then. I telephoned Tom Cooper at the British Bloodstock Agency about this. He laughed and said that he didn't have much in hand. *Red God,* a stallion that was due to be exported, was about the best of them. *Runaway Bride* visited *Red God* three times. The Aga Khan bought the first foal and Jack kept the second foal, called *Hot Shoes,* for himself. The Aga Khan also bought the third foal, a colt foal, at the Newmarket sales. That colt foal became the great *Blushing Groom! Blushing Groom* was one of the very few horses that ever won all four group one races for two-year old colts in France in the same year. The colt recorded that achievement in 1974. The horse was later syndicated for a huge amount of money and stood at stud in the U.S very successfully for several years.

Another mare that Jack acquired was one that he bought from Phil Bull called, *Diedamia.* She had a crooked leg, was very straight in front and although well bred, cost very little money. She bred two colts that turned out good winners and became sires. All the progeny were all right in conformation. This was all the more surprising because Phil Bull, the owner, who was knowledgeable about horses, had written her off in his journal.

One of her colts, *Swinging Junior,* later became a notable stallion. One day he got loose in the yard at Boyne Hill, galloped down the avenue, took a sharp right onto the road to Navan, continued down the hill towards the Boyne where he turned left at Kilcarne and headed for Navan. Shortly afterwards he was caught in the Fair Green in Navan, none the worse for his outing.

I met many nice people who came to stay at Boyne Hill and had many happy days there. We had the place in very good shape after much work. In 1972, I decided that, with my home commitments, I did not have the time to carry on looking after the place. My very good friend, Christopher Markes, took over from me.

19. Hunting, Shooting

IN THE LATE 1950s Charlie and Neenie Bird, Charlie Cameron, Lewis Doyle, Louise and myself decided we would go up to Bailieborough to have a day's hunting with the Ballymacad Hounds. The masters at the time were Tony and Elizabeth Burke. Cecil Vance, a very well known sportsman from Bailieborough, gave an excellent lawn meet. Having all enjoyed his hospitality greatly we came out and mounted our horses. We then discovered that there was no sign of the hounds or of Tony Burke. As there were no recognized coverts there we did not know where to go. We hacked around roads, but there was no sign. We saw Lewis Doyle disappearing across fields and ditches in the search. After what seemed to be a considerable time we heard a horn blowing. "I hear him", said Elizabeth and away we galloped down the road, and on coming around a corner, spotted Tony in a bog hole up to his arms in mud, blowing gone to ground! He was very irate and castigated us for not being there to pull him out. The horse and hounds were located scattered around the bog. So ended quite an adventurous day. Not much hunting but one of considerable amusement.

Hunting the hounds one day in the late nineteen fifties at Walterstown meet, although I always took the precaution of not drinking long drinks beforehand, nature called. I told the field to wait at the back of a hill while I drew below with the hounds. I was busy relieving myself when suddenly the whole lot came galloping over the hill and there I was fully exposed. After that I employed a more subtle approach, I turned my hunting horn upside down and relieved myself from the saddle! Not very hygienic but it worked when nature called.

One day, also in the late nineteen fifties when out with the Meath hounds we had an excellent hunt from Kilcarty down to the banks of the Boyne at Bective. The master,

Charlie Bird, was riding a big grey horse, which was not too brave at jumping ditches. The fox swam the river and the hounds likewise after him. Charlie rode down to the riverbank and to his consternation the horse did not stop and suddenly he found himself swimming with the horse. That was bad enough but worse was to follow. They got on to an island and by then the horse had had enough swimming and refused to proceed. Fortunately it was close to his residence, Bective House, and I had to ride madly down there and summon one of the workmen to get the boat out and proceed to the island as quickly as possible. Charlie was shivering and almost in a state of shock when he was rescued.

The sequel was also amusing. Charlie had a racehorse in training with Dan Moore and it was running that afternoon in the Fingal point-to-point at Swords. He was to ride it and it was well fancied to win. The plan was that he would pull off from the hunt halfway through and drive over to the race meeting. Of course, the long hunt and his escapade upset all this. Dan had the horse all ready for action but there was no jockey. I think they obtained a substitute at the last minute but the horse did not win and Charlie was not very popular with Dan.

Swimming with the hunting gear on is not the best occupation and of course most dangerous if you lose contact with your horse in a river of any great size. My brother-in-law, Lancelot Smith, at one time master of the Galway Blazers, had a very terrifying experience in the Claregalway River when hunting the hounds in the 1950s. Hounds were running hard and the fox and hounds crossed the river that was in flood. Lance arrived up and found a cattle crossing and jumped in. Unfortunately the current was too strong and he and his horse were swept down the river. He lost contact with his horse and surely would have drowned only he had the luck to grab a bush along the bank on his way down. Most fortunate of all, Commander Bill King, the famous sailor was out hunting that day. He immediately threw off his coat and boots and jumped in and brought Lance to safety on the far bank. The horse had clambered out further down also on the far side and between them they caught the horse, Bill managed to hoist a water- logged Lance back upon the horse and he took off and found his hounds.

It became very apparent to me that a good intelligent horse can sometimes literally save your life. One day hunting at Robinstown, Louise had a horrific fall off a bridge and into a stream that had been cleaned out in the drainage scheme. She was riding a good young horse and was just going through a gate onto the bridge over the stream when the horse in front hit it and swung it half shut. They got caught and the horse, in trying to extricate himself, fell over the side of the bridge. There was a big drop and my first impression was that Louise was killed. I leaped off my horse and ran down the stream to find that she was lying under the horse and he was standing and not in any way struggling to extricate himself. If he had done so it was inevitable that Louise would have been very badly hurt or maybe killed. The sagacity of a good animal cannot be underestimated; I reckon that he most likely saved her life.

Speaking of Robinstown meet brings to mind another rather bizarre incident. My daughter, Lorraine, was riding a very good horse; we had a check with the hounds and the horse put his head down and got a mouthful of grass. Lorraine said "You greedy horse", and went to pull away the grass hanging from his mouth whereupon he snapped at it and bit half her little finger off. Consternation and all hell arrived. Louise brought our daughter to Navan hospital and was immediately asked where the rest of her finger was. Rushing back, she found Harry Kellett who had helped and had her gloves in his pocket. On looking into them they located the piece of her finger and rushed back to the hospital for a reuniting. Lorraine recovered with no serious after effects.

Hunting is of course, a hazardous sport. During my hunting time I have had many falls but I have been lucky in that the only serious injury that I have suffered while hunting was a broken neck, which I suffered at the end of my hunting days. I remember one day hunting a horse that I had just bought from Donald Craigie. We ran out of Kilrue covert along a lane and met a fairly large ditch. I tried to jump the ditch but my horse refused twice. I had decided it was no go when my horse took off and threw me off balance. I fell down from the horse and landed heavily with the end of my spine hitting a sharp stone. I was on my own and could barely move my legs. I crawled across the field, found a gate and managed to pull myself upright with the bars of the gate. It was a considerable time before the master, Robert Elwes, appeared with my horse. He didn't believe me when I told him that I had fallen on a stone and was paralysed. "There are no stones in this field," he said. I was exceedingly sore for a week but then recovered without any more trouble.

On another day I went out riding a big horse of Charlie's. We found a fox in Piercetown covert and met a small up-fence beside the covert. My horse, we discovered afterwards, must have had something wrong with his back. Although a very good horse, up to a lot of weight, he could not get up a bank. He fell into a small ditch with his four legs in the air and I underneath him. That was not nice and the only way they got me out was to get a hold of me and every time he struggled, they pulled and got me out a little at a time. I think that they must have stretched me a bit but, miraculously, I was not hurt.

In order to hunt hounds in any way successfully, one has to have a top class horse. I have had some wonderful front-running horses and, although I was never endowed with money, I would not keep a mediocre horse, not to mention a bad one.

One of the best horses I have ever had was a horse called *Clifden*. One day I saw him hunting with the Ballymacad Hunt and made enquiries about him. I bought him from Philip Reilly from Ballyjamesduff. *Clifden* was built like a tank, was incredibly strong and although not very big, he pulled like a train. He was brilliant over any type of fence. I seldom hunted him with the foxhounds because he wanted to be nowhere except in front. At Kentstown one day I brought my daughter, Lorraine, out on her brilliant pony, *Rocket*. Lorraine's pony had a similar trait to *Clifden* in that he also pulled very hard. We found in Harristown covert. There was a large field out that day. In order to get away from the covert there was only one way out which was through a small hunting gate. As I approached the gate, I was amazed to find Lorraine right beside me with the two of us practically out of control. We went into the gate together and got stuck. For a while we couldn't go either forwards or backwards. I can say that we were not too popular with the field.

After the hunt we returned to the pub and had a couple of drinks. When I came out to go home, to my amazement, I found *Rocket* sitting in the driving seat of the horsebox! Somehow he had gotten over the partition. What a job we had to shove him out through the passenger door! Luckily, no damage was done to either pony or vehicle.

Hounds are not bred to be vicious but one must always remember that, when in a pack, and when one is on one's own with them that one must always show who is master. There is the well-known tale of a hunt kennel man who was bringing his pack on a train in England. When the train stopped at the station where he was to get off, all that was left of him were his boots!

I had one nasty experience myself. Having arranged to procure a draft of hounds in the north of Ireland, I agreed to meet them at the border and to transfer them to my hound van. A lady appeared with four and a half couple of hounds, as agreed, and I started to transfer them with a lead to my van. While I was opening the back of my van to put the fourth or fifth one in, the hound suddenly turned on me and bit me clean through the hand. I grabbed him but he turned and sunk his teeth into my other wrist. I bundled him in and said to the girl to quickly let me get the others in before I'd pass out. I managed to do this, but by the time I had the last one in I was almost gone. By great fortune, Neenie Bird had come with me and she took over. We got to the pub down the road and I had a couple of brandies and tried to wash off the blood that was all over me. She got us home and she rang for the doctor. All the fingers on both hands were paralysed for over a week but I think that I came out lucky in that I was not going around barking with rabies or some such thing.

This was a great era for shooting and fishing. I loved to walk the bogs looking for snipe and woodcock. Together with George Malcolmson, Ted Breslin and Mervyn Walker, we had many memorable days. It was not unusual to pick up forty or fifty snipe in a day. That is almost impossible to do nowadays with two or three guns. A good dog was a must. I have had some very good Labradors, all trained by Louise, who used to bring them off to pheasant shoots.

I acquired a very good Labrador line in a rather bizarre way. In the late 1950s I received a telephone call from Aer Lingus at Dublin Airport. The caller told me that my dog pup was at the airport and awaited collection by me. I explained that there must have been a mistake, as I knew nothing about a dog pup. The caller told me that it was addressed to me at Bective House. I was quite bewildered and said to Louise that I had better go and collect it anyway. He was a lovely pup.

I rang Charlie Bird in the States and asked him if he knew anything about a Labrador pup that had been sent from England. He thought about if for a while and then said, "Oh gee, we were at a dinner party in London and Mrs. Hugo Kindersley asked me if I would like to buy a Labrador pup. I asked the price." "Ten pounds", she said. "I handed over the money and completely forgot about it after that". That pup turned out to be a great dog and we had five generations of marvellous dogs from him. Hugo Kindersley was a breeder of Labradors, and his Ramhusrt breed was very good, indeed.

George, Ted and I used to go down to shoot in Kerry with my uncle, who lived at Waterville. Mostly, we went up the mountains looking for woodcock. We had some very good and successful days. In three days, we very often shot up to fifty woodcock. I remember well that on two occasions I shot the very difficult left and right, for which I got a badge and a bottle of Bols liqueur each time. This feat enabled me to become a member of the *Bols 'Sniffin' Club*. Also, I recall shooting three woodcock in as many minutes, in a little spinney up the mountains, without moving my feet. Those were good days. Unfortunately, groups of foreigners started to come in with the result that, the last year we went down there, the countryside was almost devoid of game.

20. Purchase of Asigh, Move to Asigh, Horse-breeding

AN IMPORTANT addition to the Bective property was made in November 1957, when the Asigh Farm was acquired. On the Ordnance Survey maps that give coverage to the area, Asigh is spelled, *Assey*. Mr. Bird did not like that spelling as it offended his American sensibilities, so he changed it. An ass to us is a donkey; to the Yanks it means something else. However, the origin of the name in Irish has nothing to do with donkeys or *derrieres*. Place names in Ireland that begin with As or Ass usually denote a waterfall. In this case the name does not do so but rather, means Sithe's ford. According to the Four Masters, "the battle of Ath Sithe was gained by Muircheartach (King of Ireland) against the Leinstermen, where Sithe, son of Dian was slain." That was in 524 A.D. Quite a long time ago!

Consisting of forty-five acres, and at that time, a broken down house and a small yard, it is located down-river and across the disused railway line from Bective. The purchase was not of particular relevance, but later on it proved to be a vital piece of business. The problems of trying to make some money to offset the very considerable cost of maintaining Bective were becoming acute. After various meetings, we decided to go in to the horse-breeding business. Charlie's love of horse racing was mainly of steeple-chasing but we decided that there was little gain to be had from breeding 'chasers, so we opted to breed flat racers. Our great friend Jack Parr, from Mitchelstown Stud, came over and instructed us as to the best and proper way to erect post and rail, which was essential as a first step. We cut down some oak and larch trees, got them cut to the required specifications, steeped the timber in creosote and set about our job. Meanwhile, Charlie

Rogers, who worked for Dorothy Paget, commenced to buy some brood mares for us. In our early years we had to get established and it was not until we left Bective and moved to Asigh that we made much impact with our yearling sales.

At Asigh, things began to move quite swiftly. Mr. Bird Senior rang me from the States early in 1960 to tell me that he had sold Bective to Norman Wachman but that I wasn't to worry as he intended to build a house at Asigh. In this regard, we had to select a site and to get the builders in to start the work. Building work went on apace, we erected a couple of miles of fencing and in February 1961, we moved ourselves, the horses, the lot, from Bective to Asigh.

Soon after our move we bought another farm down the road from Asigh, at Craystown, which consists of seventy-five acres. So the wonderful saga at Bective ended and we went into another era of horse breeding and cattle farming at Asigh House.

When Mr. Bird sold Bective to Norman Wachman I was a little concerned about the position regarding the kennels, which Mr. Bird had given to the Tara Harriers when I had to vacate the kennels at Bellinter. I quickly found that I need not have worried, as Norman and his wife, Maeve, were only too pleased to let us carry on as before. They were good people and had been for many years close friends of Louise and myself. Maeve had first been married to Colonel Denis Daly, the former owner of Russborough House in Co. Wicklow. Her daughter, Avia, was, and thankfully still is one of my dearest friends.

Norman carried out considerable improvements to the house. He was a very keen racing man and breeder of flat-race horses. He erected more post and rail fencing and kept from six to eight well-bred mares that he had covered by top-class stallions. Although he did not have the scale of parties that were held there during the Bird era, he nevertheless entertained his friends and gave the occasional party and dance.

Mrs. Neenie Bird and Louise Briscoe,
1955.

Charlie Bird, Junior.

Belinter House.

Bective House.

Sister Bird as a young woman.

Lorraine, Lisa and John, 1985.

George's bridge.

George and David Wilkinson at Screebe Lake, Co. Galway, 1990.

Brigadier Fowler making a presentation to George on the occasion of George's 40th season as master, 1982.

From left to right: Lelia Cooke and Louise, 2001.

Above: From left to right: Captain Simon Walford, Charlie Bird and Lord Dunsany, 1982.

From left to right: Constance, George and Stella, 2001.

Five joint masters of the Tara Harriers, 2001. From left to right: Henry Simth, Abi Hill, Lorraine McDowell, George Briscoe and Jessica Magnier.

Meath Hunt and Tara Harriers point-to-point, 2004. Presentation to Simon Walford at Rahinstown. From left to right: Simon Walford, Michael Regan, George Briscoe and Henry Reeves.

George and Avia, 1992.

Jean and George, 2005.

Jean, 2002.

Jean and George, 2005.

Paddy FitzGerald and George, 2005.

Tony Riddle-Martin who lived at Ardmulchan Castle with his wife, Sheila, were very good friends of ours. Unfortunately, their marriage broke up and eventually he and Avia got together and married. They lived for a couple of years in a nice place near Ashbourne. When they sold that they came to live in the wing at Bective where Louise and I had been living while we were there.

Norman, had a very successful shoe factory in Edenderry and used to drive there and back every day from Bective. Having more or less retired from the business and later having handed over to his sons, he and Maeve found Bective too large for them. In late 1975, I think, they sold the place to Michael Wymes, who at that time was managing director of Bula Limited, a company that owned a lead-zinc deposit on the outskirts of Navan town.

Although I had not known Michael Wymes before he bought Bective, I knew his father, Michael senior. He and I had been to shoots at Bellinter when Bill Holdsworth owned it. Michael Wymes senior was commissioner of the Garda but, having started his police career in the R.I.C., he knew my grandfather, George Heard. Michael junior did not know much about hunting but was agreeable that the hounds should stay on at Bective. Thankfully, they are there to this day.

I did not consider that Bective was large enough to have the potential to make a pheasant shoot being confined by the Trim-Navan road on one side and by the River Boyne on the other. However, Michael proved me quite wrong. He obtained a gamekeeper from England, reared a goodly number of birds and hosted one of the best small shoots in the country. The quality of the shooting was first class. Birds flew magnificently, partly because of the very large beech trees on the estate and also because of the very good stands for the guns that were positioned along the river so giving the birds elevation to get up high before being fired at. Shooting at Bective carried on for some years but unfortunately Michael has now given it up.

There being little profit to be made in conventional farming, we decided to go in for more mares upon settling in at Asigh. We kept and wintered about one hundred store cattle at Craystown, grew enough fodder for them and grew enough oats to feed and bed our horses. We decided that it would be more beneficial to sell our yearlings in Tattersalls at Newmarket, rather than at Goffs in Ireland. This may have been a correct decision at the time, but Goffs improved greatly in subsequent years and, in our latter years of breeding we moved back to Goffs.

Getting our yearlings to Newmarket in those days was quite an operation as the flying of horses was more or less in its infancy. I remember quite a number of hair-raising trips. The planes, compared to the present day, were pretty antiquated, noisy and uncomfortable. Some of the yearlings would become quite agitated and each of the bloodstock agency grooms on the plane was armed with a syringe with a big dose of sedative if a yearling became too obstructive. Our veterinary surgeon and myself did not agree to take any unnecessary risks and always gave the horses a mild sedative before leaving for the plane. This was most successful and we never had any difficulty on the journey. I do recall one instance when a yearling got so excited that we had to tie him down with ropes.

We usually flew in to Cambridge. I remember an amusing incident that happened on one of our first flights there. We landed and the pilot opened the doors and I stepped out on the tarmac whereupon a car came zooming up, out dashed a man and said," What the hell are you doing out on the runway?" I was at a loss but apparently no one was meant to leave the plane until the customs officials had arrived and cleared us to do so. I thought I was about to be arrested. We never hit any highlights in our prices for our yearlings at the venue but did breed some pretty useful racehorses in our breeding period. I name a few here: *Royal Rubicon* trained in England by Benstead and owned by Sir Charles Claque. He won some good races but usually at a long price. Every time the owner backed him at a shortish price the horse got beaten, a long price and he won. *Mary Mitsu* was a very good filly trained by Michael Kauntze in Ireland. She won listed races here and was second in the Windsor castle Stakes at Royal Ascot. She also won a good race in Epsom but got disqualified for bumping. A Japanese gentleman who lived in County Louth owned her.

Bay Empress was a top class filly that won group races and was trained by Tommy Burns for Timmy Rogers and subsequently went to stud at Airlie. *Miami Melody* was a good filly trained by John Oxx. She showed a lot of promise but unfortunately she caught a virus quite badly and never was quite the same afterwards. She was one we retained for ourselves.

The story of *Crespino* is quite extraordinary. Just before leaving for the yearling sales he put some of his innards out through his rectum. Our vet, Lewis Doyle came out and shoved them back and put a stitch to try to prevent a recurrence. I thought that that was the end of him and that he would no doubt get an infection. However, he survived. We could not send him to the sales so kept him and sent him training with Stu Murless. It was a great stroke of luck as he turned out to be a top class horse and gave Mrs. Bird and us all great excitement. He was top of the handicap on the flat and won good hurdle races and finished up as a sire and stood at Paddy Byrne's stud at Tullow. We did not possibly get enough good mares for him to cover but he was starting to get some winners when he prematurely died. He sired a prolific class winner called *Cripps* that was owned by my sister and brother-in-law, Stella and Lance Smith, and no doubt gave them a great deal of pleasure.

Jazz Musician was a nice yearling by *Jazzeiro* out of *Melodia*, a good mare that had several winners. *Jazzeiro* won the Irish 2000 Guineas. Robert Sangster owned him. We found it difficult to sell *Jazz Musician*, because its sire,

Jazzeiro, did not have many winners and his progeny became unpopular. No one would look at our yearling because of that. We knew that there was nothing wrong with him so we decided to form a small syndicate amongst ourselves. This again proved great luck. He was trained by Michael Kauntze, won some good races and was fourth in the Coventry Stakes at Royal Ascot. He gave us great fun, paid for all his expenses and left us with a nice sum of money when he was sold to someone in the USA.

The last one I shall mention is *Dr Leunt*. He was by a sprinting sire out of *Not Mistaken*, a *Mill Reef* mare. He did not have any distinction on the flat but showed great promise over hurdles and came in second in the four year-old Champion Hurdle at Cheltenham but was subsequently disqualified for having gone the wrong side of a flag. However, he was then purchased by English trainer Philip Hobbs and became a top class chaser. Never having run a bad race in big chases, it was sad when he dropped dead at his best.

21. Purchase of Boyne Bridge, Hunting

IN THE MEANTIME, we had been working very hard at Asigh and Craystown. All the necessary stud paling had been done; the stables and George Bell's house in the yard at Asigh had been completed. With the help of Charlie Rogers, we bought in six more mares in order to keep the business rolling. Craystown land was greatly improved by fertilizing and by fencing. We grew oats and hay there for the horses.

The old railway line from Navan to Kilmessan, which was discontinued in 1963, ran beside Asigh and over a very fine bridge on the River Boyne. One day I saw two men walking back and over the bridge and then down beneath it, regarding the structure. I went out and said, "Can I help you?" They told me that they were just looking to see where they would have to place explosives in order to blow it up, which, they said that they would have to do, in order to avoid liability in the event of accidents. I said, "That would be a great pity. Would you ever consider selling it?" They looked at me as if were a bit of a nut and told me that no one had ever asked them about buying a bridge from them before. However, one of them said, "I suppose we could sell it to you." The big question then was how much. They retired for a while, ruminated and returned. "Would sixty pounds be too much?" one of them enquired. I almost shook their hands off and so acquired one of the finest bridges on the Boyne for a nominal sum!

Hunting with the Taras was progressing very well. Joe Moorehead, who had been joint master with me for some years, retired in 1962, when I was joined by Captain Simon Walford. We were starting to expand our country to the west towards the Westmeath border and to the north into Cavan.

This was working out well and relieving the pressure of too much hunting from our original country.

As my joint masters Joe Moorehead, Simon Walford, John Bryce-Smith and Leslie Johnson hunted hounds in the Longwood end of the country; I was able to do a considerable amount of hunting with the Meath Foxhounds. For two periods over sixteen years I was, in fact, chairman of the Meaths. In the first period, my brother-in-law, Lance Smith was joint master with Elizabeth Burke. We had a lot of great sport. Indeed, at that time, it could have been said of me that I was living the life of Reilly! Sport and enjoyment with the harriers were excellent. I have always considered that time as a great period in my life.

Leslie Johnson was a businessman who bought Moyrath Castle, Kildalkey, and moved over from England to live here. He had little experience of horses and hunting but, when Simon Walford retired, he agreed to come in to fill his place. His daughter, Sandra, married John Bryce-Smith, who carried the horn until Leslie's untimely death in 1976. He died in the saddle, hunting with the Meath hounds, which was a great shock, as he had been hunting with the harriers the day before and was in great form.

We had many amusing incidents with Leslie, one of which I shall relate: one day we all arrived at a meet and went into the pub for a drink. On coming out, Leslie let down the ramp of his horsebox but there was no horse inside. "Eh," said he. "Where's the bloody 'orse?" "You mustn't have put him in", I said. He was sure that he had. "If so, he must have been spirited away," said I. It transpired that he had not tied up the horse properly and that, when travelling, the horse turned around in the box and jumped over the back ramp. Later on, the horse was found in a bog about seven miles from the meet, without a scratch on him.

Leslie never liked doing things by halves. When he bought Moyrath, he first decided to have sheep. He had thousands of them. Shortly afterwards, he decided to give up the sheep and bought hundreds of cattle. Cattle-farming lasted a while until he went into horses and brood mares. He had stallions, brood mares, foals and horses of all ages, racehorses and hunters. That was quite an operation!

Leslie had two daughters in England by his first wife, who unfortunately died young. He was married again over here to Mairead, with whom he had six more daughters. At the time when his last daughter was due, he had a good horse running in a big race in England. He said to our local vet, Lewis Doyle, that it would be a great double for him if his wife had a son and if his horse were to win in England. His wife had another daughter and his horse was beaten. When the pair met again Lewis said, "Horse had two stones too many and baby had two stones too few".

The fishing in general was starting to decline at the end of the 1960s. Pollution was taking its toll on rivers and lakes and over-netting at sea was decimating the Atlantic salmon. Trawlers in Burtonport, county Donegal, were bringing in thousands of salmon from their miles of monofilament nets out at sea. This could not last and is now illegal. Unfortunately, to a large extent, the damage has been done and it is now a matter of survival for the Atlantic salmon.

After the death of Leslie Johnson, I was joined in the mastership by my cousin, Susan Lanigan O'Keeffe and, shortly afterwards, by Commander Collard. After this, it became necessary for me to hunt the hounds in both ends of the country, which obviously meant much more involvement for me. Because of this I had less time to hunt with the foxhounds, an experience that I greatly enjoyed when I had less responsibility upon my shoulders.

22. Greek Holidays

I HAVE not really travelled very much, however, I have made a couple of memorable trips to Syros and Crete. The first of these was a visit to Crete in the 1960s with Louise, my sister, Stella, and brother-in-law, Lance Smith. We stayed in a very comfortable hotel on the seaside near Heraklion. The flight out was quite memorable as the pilot asked me up to the cockpit, which I found very interesting, particularly observing the landing at Heraklion airport. We knew the pilot, Jock Armstrong, very well as he hunted with us regularly.

We visited the ruins at Knossis and I was most intrigued to see the first ever known water closet. It was fed from a stream coming down the mountain and had a run off which did not appear to be leaving any pollution. The following day the girls went in to Heraklion to do some shopping. Lance and I decided we would climb the mountain behind our hotel which did not seem very formidable, but we fairly soon found that this was not at all the case. I made the stupid mistake of setting off in shorts and very soon realized that the mountain contained many whin bushes, which were exceedingly prickly. Having climbed for quite a time the summit still looked a long way up. Lance wished to give up but I considered that, having gone so far that I would go on to the top. We agreed and eventually reached our objective. The view was spectacular and we spent a while enjoying it. There is little dusk there so it becomes dark from daylight very quickly. I looked at my watch and said we had better get going quickly. About half way down and the daylight failing, Lance's braces gave up and that completely slowed up our progress as he was holding up his trousers with one hand. I said, "If necessary take them off, we shall never get off the mountain if the light fails and I don't' relish spending the night up here." We stumbled down the last bit and by Jove, we were ready for a drink after that episode. Needless to say my legs were torn and ripped. I got great relief next day lying in the salt water, which took a lot of the pain from them.

Next day Louise and I took a plane to Athens, on our way to stay in Syros with great friends John and Aliki Wills. We got to Piraeus where we stayed the night at a small hotel on the harbour front. I struggled down to the harbour carrying two large cases. I bought our tickets along a wall facing many boats. There was a crowd of people shouting and roaring in Greek, which was pretty intimidating and frustrating. I eventually found one with Syros written up and bought two tickets. Although I did not know the charge for the tickets, I considered I had paid a pretty hefty price. We boarded the boat with a sigh of relief but that was not the end. A sailor appeared who spoke English and I quickly discovered that we were on the wrong boat. We did then find the right one and I later discovered the reason why the fare was so large. I had purchased a ticket not only for ourselves but also for a car!

We had a pleasant trip out to Syros and stayed in a lovely new house on a hill overlooking the sea with John and Aliki. When we arrived John was in a somewhat disturbed state and I asked Aliki what was wrong. "Well," she said, "we have a well-known American nuclear scientist and his wife staying with us. They went off for a walk this morning and it is now well into the afternoon and John thinks that he has been abducted by the Russians!" I thought, "My goodness, could this be so?" John became more and more agitated as time went on and rang the U.S. embassy in Athens. Next thing a boat appeared in the bay and weighed anchor. John said, "I knew it! There is a Russian boat about to take them away!" Things were getting serious and it was almost dark when the two appeared and said they had a lovely walk all around the island!

On another occasion we went for a drive and were up on a hill overlooking the harbour. There seemed to be very queer antics going on and Aliki asked an old fellow with a donkey and cart what it was all about. Apparently a boat was coming in and another leaving and they ran into each other. It transpired that the two captains hated each other and neither would give way when they met and very considerable damage was done to both vessels.

My old school friend from Woodlands preparatory school days, the late Sir Richard Musgrave and his wife, Maria, had a most attractive house built right on the southern end of the island overlooking the sea. Louise and I went out to see them in the seventies. It was so pleasant and entertaining to visit them. People of means, mostly Americans, used to rent the house for a period during the summer.

We went to visit for drinks one evening and I being an Irish whiskey-drinker was quite put out when I found I could not obtain Irish whiskey on the island. Dick said to me "I shall give you some Irish whiskey on condition you entertain my guests and sing them some songs." I obliged and the more Irish whiskey I consumed, the more vocal I became.

Sir Richard's sister, Lisanne, also had a house on the island. She asked us to a lunch' party. We duly appeared and were quite amazed and out of our depth when we found ourselves rubbing shoulders with a mass of hippies. We tried to behave normally but were certainly put back a peg when we got talking to a rather scruffy couple. They announced that they got married that morning. "Oh," I asked, "are your parents over?" "Oh, not at all, we don't' bother about them!" I said to Louise you learn something every day.

Syros is a lovely island, we loved it and I hope I shall go back to visit it again some day.

23. Fishing in Canada

When on a visit to Charlie and his present wife, Sister, in the 1970s, I was invited by a man called Den Russell to go fishing for salmon on a famous river in Canada called the Restiquache, that flows into the Gulf of St. Lawrence.

I boarded a small plane in Boston that took me to Presque Isle in Maine where I was met by Den. From there we drove to the Canadian border where I was brought into a back room and interrogated and searched. I did not know for what reason but I realised later that having an Irish passport and with the troubles raging with the I.R.A. in Northern Ireland that they were suspicious of any Irishman. Anyway, I was released after about fifteen minutes and then we set off and drove through dense forests for a hundred miles or more. The vastness of the country with little or no habitation is remarkable.

We stayed in a magnificent lodge out in the wilds on the bank of the river. The food and hospitality were wonderful. The main owner of the syndicate was a Bobby Goodyear who was a delightful person.

In order to combat poaching no one was allowed to fish from the bank. The procedure was to fish from a canoe that was usually manned by two Indians. My two locals were grand fellows and we had a lot of fun and laughter together. Although the water level in the river was exceedingly low for the time of year when we were there, there was a good number of salmon around. For conservation purposes, with fish numbers falling every year, we had to return to the water any fish that we landed. Having connected with quite a few fish, I must say that I had some misgivings when having to return a fish weighing thirty-two pounds to the water.

One day when the river was very clear and when little action was taking place, my Indian pals said, "We shall try a bit of kedging.' "What is that?" I enquired. There was a demonstration for me. The procedure entailed getting over a pool where you could see the salmon under the water and then dropping down slowly a tubed badger fly among them. It was a like a parachute going down. To my surprise, a fish grabbed it straight away. When this occurred one had to strike at once or one would fail to hook the fish. This is in contrast to what one does when normally fishing with a fly. If one strikes too quickly, one invariably fails to hook the fish. The first fish that we hooked ran hard up the river, jumped and got away. After this I let the fly down again. The same thing happened again as a fish grabbed it. We had better luck this time as we managed to land our prey.

At that time the fishing laws were very strictly enforced with watchers placed along the riverbank. One day Bobby Goodyear and a friend of his were fishing in a canoe when the lodge manager came down from his house and told him that he was wanted on the telephone. While he was gone, his friend got out onto the bank and commenced to fish. Within a very short time a bailiff came across the river and proceeded to confiscate his rod and reel. I bet that Bobby's friend felt sorry for himself!

Returning to Ipswich, Massachusetts, we drove down an eight-lane freeway that runs from Canada all the way down to Florida. Those journeys are most boring, as one gets very little by way of views of scenery. Many cars over there have an automatic speed control which means that all one has to do is to set the throttle at the appropriate speed and steer the car. Each state has its own speed limit so that the speed control mechanism had to be adjusted accordingly.

One incident I remember was indeed quite bizarre. We pulled into a filling station and shop along the highway. Having done our business, Den got in and drove off, I sitting in front beside him. He was just about to enter the motorway when I said, "Where is Lilly?"

She had been sitting in the back and Den thought she was there when he drove off. If we had got on to the highway it would have taken a long time to have driven back and God knows how long she would have been stranded there at the petrol station. However, we returned and picked Lilly up and all was well.

24. The Passing of Mr. And Mrs. Bird

SADLY, Mr. Bird senior died in 1980 while over visiting at Asigh. He was ninety-six years old but was wonderfully clear in all his actions right up to the end. He was a magnificent gentleman of the old school and I owe him and his dear wife, Julia, so much in making my life so happy and prosperous.

Shortly after he had arrived at Asigh he got a bad cold which got progressively worse. Later, he fell into a coma. Just before this came about, he asked me what I was doing. I told him that I was going down to try for a fish on the river. He went into a coma for a couple of days and when he momentarily came out of it he said to the nurse, "Did George catch a fish?"

On account of the difficulty of shipping the body back to the United States, it was decided that his body should be cremated. At that time, there was no crematorium in the Republic, so he had to be brought to Belfast. Charlie Bird and Waring Willis went up a couple of days later to collect his ashes, which had been placed in an urn, which was then put into a cardboard box. On their way home, they decided to stop off at the Maze races that were taking place on that day. On reaching the Border, a customs officer enquired as to what was in the box and asked Charlie to open it. Charlie said to him, "Oh that's only my father. We brought him racing today." Julia Bird, who was most wonderful and composed, was greatly amused.

Sometime in the 1970s, Mr. Bird, when looking at his horse, *Crespino*, which was in training with Stu Murless at the time, had a bad fall and broke his hip. He was brought off to hospital in Dublin where the orthopaedic surgeon there was not very hopeful of his recovery because at the time, Mr. Bird, was coming into his ninetieth year. However, he confounded everyone and made a complete recovery in a reasonably short time.

It so happened that the horse was starting his racing career at the time of Mr. Bird's accident. The horse was very good and won some top races on the flat and later became a top class hurdler. Mrs. Bird and I had some great trips to various meetings around the country to watch him run. He was running one day in the Galway hurdle. On going into the enclosure I said to Mrs. Bird that she should go in through the owners' and trainers' entrance as I had to go further down to pay to get in. "No way," she said and marched up to the owners' and trainers' entrance and, in a loud voice said, "Mr. and Mrs. Bird." If I was Mr. Bird the officials must have thought that I was her toy boy.

Mrs. Bird owned a very successful chasing mare called *Heartbreak Hill* that won many top races. In the 1932 Grand National she started as favourite and was going beautifully until coming to Valentine's Brook where a loose horse baulked her. She turned and finished in sixth place but probably would have won if she hadn't been interfered with.

Mrs. Bird tried through three generations of horses to breed anything of any import on the racecourse but was unsuccessful. When all seemed lost the great granddaughter of *Heartbreak Hill*, *Argilla*, arrived on the scene. She was just in training but did no good on the track. In the meantime, *Crespino* was sent to stud and we decided to send *Argilla* to be covered by him. She produced a big, strong colt that Julia named *Hill Cry*. As a four year old we hunted him a few times and then sent him into training with John Bryce-Smith. He turned out to be a brilliant jumper and proceeded to win five heavy weight point-to-point races. His prospects as a top chaser looked very good and we were all most excited about it. However, fate moved in again on the down side. He started to jump badly with none of his old ability. Eventually it was discovered he had contracted brucellosis and our vet said that we might as well forget about racing but that he might make a hunter. What a hunter he proved to be! Terry Dowdall hunted hounds on him for years and many people said he was the best thoroughbred hunter that they had ever seen in Meath.

We had a visit in 1980 of Jack Lemmon, his wife Felicia, and his daughter, Courtney, who stayed for a few days. They were most delightful people. I brought Jack to Navan one day to do some shopping and people kept stopping me in the street and saying, "Is that Jack Lemmon?" We decided to get him to buy one of our yearling fillies that we sent to my cousin, Aubrey Brabazon to be trained. Aubrey said the first thing to be done is to name her. They called her *Cookie Puss*. I always said name a horse well and it will often prove good. This was a dubious start and as we feared she proved no good on the racecourse. However, Felicia and Courtney were often to be found in the stable petting her and saying, "*Cookie Puss*, we love you". They certainly must have as they shipped her to California and history does not relate what happened to her afterwards.

1980 was a sad year for me, as coming after the death of Mr. Bird, my beloved cousin, George Malcolmson, died aged 70. As I have previously stated he was much more a brother than a cousin to me and to this day I miss him greatly. He was an enormously popular man in the sporting world and a great loss.

The next important event in our lives was the marriage of our daughter, Lorraine, to John McDowell. This was a very happy occasion and united two well-known families in Meath. They had both been to St Columba's School so certainly must have known each other well before they took the plunge. The first three years of their married life they spent in the lovely old cottage on our farm at Craystown. John and his cousin, Peter, own McDowell's jewellers in O'Connell Street, Dublin. The business is known as *The Happy Ring House*.

Sadly, in February 1983, I got news from Charlie that his mother, Julia, had died. It was imperative that Louise and I got over to her funeral in Ipswich, Massachusetts. On arrival to stay with Charlie and Sister I was asked if I would say a few words about Julia at the burial service. This I considered a great honour as I had such tremendous respect and love for so fine a person.

I cannot speak highly enough of the qualities of Julia Bird. From the time that I took over the running of Bective until her death, when we were at Asigh, she had been almost like a mother to me. People who did not know her well were in awe of her as she was very regal and took no nonsense from anyone. Mrs. Bird was very intelligent and had a great knowledge and appreciation of the arts. In her lifetime she collected many valuable paintings with which she adorned her homes.

Her integrity was complete and always I enjoyed her absolute trust and loyalty. I used to enjoy immensely driving her to various places around the country whenever her horses were running in races there. When she had *Crespino* at stud at Tullow in County Carlow we used to go down there to see how things were progressing.

When Bective was sold she expressed misgivings about it and stated that she didn't think that she would come back to Ireland anymore. When we took up residence at Asigh, she rather reluctantly came back to Ireland. After a short while she grew to love the place and we saw her more often than in previous times.

Having come from a well-known and wealthy family in Massachusetts, she knew many people in diplomatic circles and very many of the Irish aristocracy. A eulogy that I read at her funeral conveyed the warmth of feeling felt for her by all her friends in Ireland.

Charlie did not come over a great deal after Julia's death and we started to run down our horse breeding and farming operation. Later in that year the members and friends of the

Tara Harriers gave me a presentation of some wonderful Waterford cut glass for having been forty years as joint-master and huntsman of the pack. Louise was presented with a lovely painting of the Twelve Pins in recognition of her twenty-five years as secretary and field-master. The editor of *Horse and Hounds*, Michael Clayton, came over and hunted with us and wrote a very good article for the magazine.

Also, the photographer, Jim Meads, ran with the hunt and took many excellent photos of the day's sport. Louise and I were greatly honoured by the generosity of all our sporting friends.

In 1985 Charlie decided that, as he did not come over very much that he was considering selling Asigh. This decision was made all the easier when John and Lorraine intimated that they would like to buy the place. Everything was agreed and then with the wonderful Bird generosity, Charlie said that we would do up the cottage at Craystown and that Louise and I could retire and live there. Architects were brought in and as it did not appear feasible to successfully build onto the cottage, Charlie said that we would build a new house. This is how our lovely home, Craystown House, came to be built. We moved to Craystown in 1985.

Lorraine and John lived at the cottage at Craystown for about three years. When Charlie decided to build a new house at Craystown with the intention that we'd move from Asigh, John asked me one day if Charlie would ever think of selling Asigh. I put this to Charlie and Charlie agreed. I am not privy to the terms but I know that he treated them well. When the sale was agreed, Doreen, John's late mother, came in on it too. That is to say, Doreen and John bought the place between them. Doreen moved into the stud groom's house which we had built in the nineteen sixties. Doreen had been living at Ardbraccan Lodge, outside Navan but she found that it was too big for her, being on her own, so she sold it.

25. Others we Loved

A DEAR FRIEND of ours was Lelgarde Evans. She was a daughter of Lord St. David's. We first got to know her and her husband, Colin, when they bought a farm at Kilmartin and came to live there. Colin, always known as 'Tinker,' was a rear gunner during the war in a Lancaster bomber. It must have been one of the most dangerous jobs in the war.

Tinker got in with Dan Moore, a famous horse trainer, and got Lelgarde to purchase a few horses. You can't have racehorses without shelling out money. The horses didn't work out and, under economic pressure they sold Kilmartin and moved to Monkstown in Dublin before coming to the townland of Ardsallagh across the River Boyne from Bellinter House.

The land that they bought down by the Boyne was originally Bellinter land and then was sold to the Land Commission. My father paid the Land Commission an annual rent for the land. However, my father had so much land at that time that he did not have any use for this piece and so he sub-let it to Pat Sheridan of Navan. Then, sometime in the nineteen fifties, I think, an Act was introduced whereby the person renting land from the Land Commission could buy it out. My father said, "Oh, yes, well I'll buy it." "Oh, you won't," said the Land Commission, "You have sub-let it." So they sold it to Pat Sheridan instead.

There were beautiful beech trees on the land, all the way up the river for a mile and a half. My father knew Pat Sheridan very well and was anxious about the long beech wood opposite Bellinter House. He got word that Pat Sheridan was going to fell the wood so he went to see him. Pat Sheridan said, "Oh, I wouldn't do that, I wouldn't do that." "Alright," said my father. After a while there was crash, bang, wallop as Sheridan began to cut the whole wood down. It was a sacrilege as the beeches were not very old, having been planted in my grandfather's time.

Shortly afterwards when the tree stumps had been cleared away and the land sown with grass, Lelgarde and Tinker bought the land from Pat Sheridan and had a house built on the property. There were forty five to fifty acres in that strip of land, which ran from Bellinter Bridge up to near Asigh. This must have been in the early fifties. In the winter time the land was like a lake when the River Boyne flooded. That was common until the River Boyne was drained.

The drainage of the River Boyne commenced at Bellinter Bridge in 1969. I well remember the Minister for Posts and Telegraphs, Michael Hilliard, a local man, performing the opening. Having said some suitable words regarding the enterprise, he then pronounced the commencement of the project by pressing down on a lever to detonate explosives that had been placed in the water up-river. Lelgarde, whose house was not far from the bank of the river nearby, was quite amazed to have suddenly and unexpectedly heard a great explosion and to have seen one of her windows fall in.

Mr. Bird owned land that extended for about one and a half miles along the north bank of the river. Previously, this had been Belllinter land. Mr. Bird had bought it from Lelgarde Evans at the time that he had Asigh House built in the 1960s. Therefore, we were the first landowners on whose land the drainage scheme had begun.

During the drainage works, large heaps of rock, sand, silt, earth and debris were thrown upon the bank of the river. We were left with the problem of disposal. We decided to spread it out onto the contiguous fields but in places there was not enough topsoil to cover it over. The job was completed but not at all satisfactorily. As the project progressed up-river farmers got wise to the problem associated with spoil-spreading and they insisted that trenches should be dug wherein the spoil was dumped and covered with top-soil. This method of disposal and reclamation was completely successful.

Tinker was involved with horses, spending money. He was in with all the racing people. They had been there a few years when the Russell Arms Hotel in Navan came on the market. Lelgarde and Tinker decided to buy it. After having purchased it, Lelgarde managed it. She told me herself that she could have made a good success of it but that the position was hopeless. She couldn't do audits or stock-taking because Tinker used to come in and take all the money out of the till and take bottles to various people. She never knew where she was! He had mucked the whole bloody thing up. In 1966 their marriage broke up and Tinker moved away.

One time at a party in Lelgarde and Tinker's house near Bellinter Bridge a ruction broke out. Dan Moore, the horse trainer, did not like beards. Whenever he had a few drinks and if he was near a bearded man, he would pluck a few hairs from that man's beard. I don't know how he wasn't killed for this carry on. Well, the row started when Dan Moore pulled a hair out of Holdsworth's beard. It got worse and worse after that. Iny Willis took off her shoe and hit somebody over the head with it. I don't know who the receiver was. A lot of drink had been taken at that stage. Someone else had his shirt ripped off. After a while it settled down and peace and amiability were restored.

When Tinker departed, Lelgarde was left with hardly any money and with a mortgage on the property which she had to service. We all knew of her plight. One day at Asigh Mrs. Bird took me aside to ask me about Lelgarde. I told her that her situation was pretty dire, whereupon she took out a chequebook, wrote a cheque and told me to go straight away to a bank in Navan and to lodge the cheque to Lelgarde's account and that I was not to tell anybody about the matter. Well, I can say that the cheque was a large one! It was another gesture of the magnificent Bird generosity. Lelgarde was able to pay off her mortgage, to later sell the place and to have a little cottage built for herself and to have some money in the bank.

Lelgarde had a very distressing experience when she was young. She was out yachting with her boyfriend and a male friend of her boyfriend. And whatever happened, whether it was a squall or something else, the boat was up-ended. She was a very strong swimmer and tried to help them. Unfortunately, both men were lost. She managed to get to the shore to raise the alarm. I suppose that must have affected her all her life.

During the war years she volunteered to drive a lorry in which she carried spare parts for aircraft to the different airfields around the southern half of England. At that time she was very friendly with David Niven, the late, well-known actor.

Lelgarde was a great character and a great raconteuse. She was a lovely lady and always full of fun. We were all very sad when she died in 1984.

Lelgarde's younger son, Roland is a fine young man and has a lovely wife, Anette. I met them both recently at a lunch' party. I have always liked Roland. He also went to my old school, Portora.

Ronnie, Louise's brother, taught English at the Bluecoat school, Blackhall Place in Dublin and continued to teach when the school moved out to Palmerstown where it is known as King's Hospital School. He was a very interesting character and a great traveller. He loved islands. He travelled to Iceland, to the Azores, to the Canaries, to the Shetlands, to the Faroes and God knows where else.

When he retired from teaching, Charlie Bird very kindly gave him a little plot of land at Craystown upon which he had a house built. He wanted to have a wooden house built on the site but I dissuaded him of this idea and, instead, he had a concrete house built, which I think was much better. Ronnie was a very bright and interesting man and he particularly liked Lelgarde. Both were well read and had a fair knowledge of Spanish. They used to talk about everything together over a few glasses of gin and tonic.

After Lelgarde's funeral service at Bective church in May 1984, Ronnie went home and had quite a few drinks to drown his sorrows. After that he drove off to get more drink, I think. Coming up to Connell's Cross on the Navan-Trim road he crashed into a tree. The front of the car was smashed and the windscreen was broken. Paddy Ryall who lives there opposite the tree, went out when he heard the bang, found Ronnie and drove him back to Craystown, first having taken the keys out of the ignition switch. Ronnie had a spare set of keys and shortly after Paddy Ryall had left him home, he walked the mile and a half back to the car and drove down to the nearest place where he could buy liquor. That evening when Ronnie was abroad, Louise and I were going out to dinner somewhere and as we were driving down near Connell's Cross I saw this car with a smashed windscreen and dents on the front and side coming towards us. "My God," I said to myself, "That's Ronnie." I was hoping that Louise hadn't seen him but she had. "My God," she said, "What's he at now?" And there he was with no windscreen and the whole thing bashed in. I don't think that he ever drove again after that.

Charlie Bird and Sister were over shortly after that. I said that I wanted to go to Flynns' of Summerhill to buy a few plants. They said that they would like to come along with me. I said that that was fine. Ronnie said that he would like to come too and asked me if I would pick him up. When I went down to Ronnie's house all I could see was blood everywhere. I went in and found Ronnie in bed. "What happened?" I said. "Oh, I got a fall," said Ronnie. "My God," I said, "It must have been an awful fall." Ronnie had planned to go on a trip to Austria within a few days and was quite put out about it. He said to me, "Don't tell Louise, don't tell Louise." "Begod," said I, "I don't know about that." There was a big gash on his head and blood all over his face and neck. I went out to the car and told Charlie and Sister that Ronnie wasn't coming with us as he had a fall. So off we went. On the way back I called in to see him. He was still in bed and told me not to tell Louise. I said to Ronnie that I had to tell her. Down Louise goes and finds such a mess! Poor Ronnie didn't go on his trip to Austria. Well, he wasn't fit to travel, he was *hors de combat*.

Another time I went down to Ronnie and he told me that he was on the dry. I went in and Ronnie had a two-litre box of wine with a tap in it on a sideboard. "Begod, Ronnie," said I, "I thought that you were on the dry." "Oh, so I am," said Ronnie. " Well, what about that?" said I, pointing at the box of wine. "Oh that, wine doesn't count, wine doesn't count," said he.

Ronnie was a very highly respected teacher of English and indeed I met some of his pupils from time to time and they could not speak highly enough of his ability and personality. On his retirement he had held the position of deputy head of the school. I know that he had a great ability to impart his considerable knowledge to others, an ability that makes a good teacher.

I consider that in the present day it is not easy for teachers. It is almost impossible for them to impose discipline. If they so much as touch a child they risk the possibility of being sued. In my school days if we misbehaved we got a few strokes of the cane. We never held any resentment. I do remember one time going to visit Ronnie and when going up to his room a young boy ran up the stairs and in front of him. He grabbed him and gave him a kick in the backside and said, "Report to me in the morning." How things have changed! Ronnie was an institution in King's Hospital and is fondly remembered by many.

The last time that I was with Ronnie was one morning in the late nineteen eighties when I was going to Kilmessan and I picked him up to take him for a bit of shopping. Everything was fine and Ronnie appeared to be well. After our little outing in Kilmessan I dropped him back to his house. After lunch' Louise dropped down to see how he was and went in and called, "Ronnie, Ronnie, where are you?" There was no reply. She looked around and there in his bedroom he was stone dead. Poor Ronnie. He must have had a big heart attack for he was all right in the morning.

In 1987 an old school pal and a great friend of mine, Waring Willis, died. We had many great times together. He was always on for fun. Sadly, his widow, Iny, another great friend, was killed in a motoring accident in Northern Ireland in late 1991. Within a few years we had lost four of our dear ones. They will always be missed.

The worst and saddest day of my life was 22nd September, 2001 when my dear Louise dropped dead. I was devastated.

We had been watching Ireland playing Scotland in the Six Nations Championship on television. The match had been deferred from the early part of the year because of the outbreak of foot and mouth disease in cattle and sheep in Britain. We were being beaten and eventually lost to the Scots. During the first half of the match, Louise said to me that she felt a bit breathless. I said to her that she wasn't to worry too much about it and to take it easy and that it would pass off. She got up and said that she was going for a rest. At half time in the match I got up and walked around to see how she was when I found her dead on the bedroom floor. It was a horrible shock.

Dear Louise had not been in good health for some time and suffered greatly from osteo-arthritis. It was so distressing for me to see her in such pain and knowing that there was no cure or respite. As well as that, she had become very forgetful. She used to become very frustrated when doing the

Harriers' books because she had always been efficient in running things and was able to make out accounts. Towards the end, in doing the hunt accounts, she would say, "Oh, I'm no use, why can't I do this now?" She was becoming rapidly worse and couldn't remember things and so forth. I came to accept that it was a merciful release for her when she passed away. I missed her so much and the suddenness of it all was a terrible blow. However, with the great support of my relatives and close friends, I gradually accepted my loss and survived the dreadful ordeal.

However, life must continue. I was so fortunate in having a great friend of mine and of Louise, in Jean Wilson. About two or three days after Louise's funeral she came over to Craystown to see how I was and said that she would come over some evening and cook something for me. Her late husband, Jimmy, had passed away in 1994 and it was so wonderful for me when I received such support from her in my hour of need. I have known Jean's family, the Craigies, all my life and I have known Jean since before she married Jimmy Wilson, but maybe not all that well at that time. Of course, I got to know her very well when she married Jimmy because Jimmy was a friend of mine. We used to see them every so often at parties, dinners and hunt balls.

Since I had known Jean very well and was fond of her, I became fonder of her after that because she is a lovely person and a very good woman. After that we began to see a lot of each other and to go out together. Soon afterwards we discovered that we were very happy in each other's company and that we loved each other. I know that it wasn't long after poor Louise's death and, perhaps, it didn't look at all well; however, that is the nature of things. Apart from anything else, our relationship enabled me to get over Louise's death and to build a new life. I know that Louise would have been happy with that.

Shortly after dear Louise had passed away, two more of my

dearest friends, Jim and Jill McAleese, to the grief of their many friends, also departed this world. They were both much too young and good to have gone so soon.

Jim was a schoolteacher by profession and I first got to know him in the 1960s when he was teaching English at Headford School, Kells. Teaching was just one of his many great attributes; he was also a great leader. He was always the instigator of songs and stories at parties and generally was a man to get things going and to create fun.

Jim was a keen sportsman and his main love in country field sports was otter hunting. He kept his own pack of otter hounds. Even if otter hunting was a bit slow at times when out near the river, it was never boring as the atmosphere was always great and at times was hilarious.

For fifty years I had parties when I was master and huntsman of the Tara Harriers. At many of those functions, Jim was always a wonderful master of ceremonies. In our former home, Bellinter House, Louise and I threw parties to celebrate my seventieth birthday, our fiftieth wedding anniversary and my eightieth birthday. Jim presided at each of those parties and as usual did a great job.

Jim started a gardening group some years ago that he called "Dig it and dung it" which had great success. With the group he visited gardens around Ireland and England and had a great time of it. Even though the group continues in its activities and is a very successful and happy bunch, the loss of Jim has left a void.

Jill came from Co. Wicklow and I first met her when she was riding mistress at Headford School. That was in the nineteen sixties. Working at Headford brought Jim and Jill together to form such a lovely partnership and family. Jill hunted with the Meath Foxhounds and with the Tara Harriers. I had many happy days hunting with her.

One day Commander Collard, then joint master of the Tara Harriers, collected Jill and her horse to go to attend a meet at Tierworker, in Cavan country. On arriving there it was snowing heavily and there was a little snow lying on the ground. Because of the conditions, which were getting worse, we had to abandon the hunt and adjourned to a pub. After some time, 'Pinkie,' as Commander Collard was known, set of for home with Jill. However, on the way, because of the condition of both the weather and of 'Pinkie,' they found themselves upended in a ditch in the wilds of Cavan. Neither person nor animal was hurt but it was very late when they arrived home. I don't know if Jim thought that his wife had eloped with the commander.

The end for them was very sad. Jill developed cancer and Jim, of course, was greatly distressed by this unfortunate event. Jim fell ill and entered hospital for a minor operation. To the consternation of all his family and friends, he died unexpectedly. Jill suffered on in her condition but became progressively worse and passed away not long after Jim in 2003.

26. Shooting

ICONTINUED to do some shooting but unfortunately my eyesight deteriorated and I got to the stage, to the disgust of my Labradors, that I could not shoot anything. A few years ago I had cataracts removed from my eyes and now I can see a lot better and can shoot an odd snipe and woodcock.

Dr Oliver Chance took over forestry in Moyode beside Athenry in the 1920s. He ran it very successfully as a woodcock shoot for many years. In the 1940s some of his friends came in and formed a syndicate, which survives to this day. I first shot there in the mid 1960s and became a member of the syndicate in the early 1970s. We have 9 to 10 guns and shoot it on three weekends in the season.

Although we had some great bags through the years what I really enjoyed was the difficulty of shooting the birds. I always felt that they had a very good chance of getting away which was so much more sporting and one felt one had achieved something in shooting a few birds there.

For some years we also rented the shooting at Lough Cutra. Both places during the 1970s and 1980s held a great number of woodcock and we had some memorable days. Since then, however, it has deteriorated. We used to be able to get up to 18 beaters, which were essential as many of the woods are very large. We can now only get 5 or 6 young lads and many of our woods have become impenetrable with briars so we are to a great degree dependent on dogs and the hard work of some of our younger members. The weather has also a great deal to do with amounts of birds arriving in our country, as they are almost all migratory coming from Norway, Russia and the Arctic Circle primarily. The so-called global warming I think is also reducing the number of birds coming to our shores. We all stay in the Newpark Hotel, Athenry and the parties and fun are of the highest order. I was greatly honoured by our fellow members a few years ago in being made an honorary member of the club. My contribution to the bag is very little now but I greatly enjoy the outings.

When the disaster occurred at the nuclear power station at Chernobyl in the former Union of Soviet Socialist Republics in early 1986, radioactive fall-out in Western Europe from the explosion was first detected in Scandinavia. Later on it was shown that particles from the event had spread as far west as Ireland. However, as the woodcock we shoot migrate from Scandinavia, some people were saying at the time that it might be unsafe to eat the birds. Well, I have eaten them as have lots of people and I am not going about glowing.

On another occasion in the west of Ireland in the early 1980s I was shooting with my great friend, Christopher Markes, in a forest up the Inagh valley. We called to a farmer and asked his permission to shoot a small wood just off the road, which was willingly given. Christopher said to me "Go down that old lane and I shall beat it with my spaniels." I proceeded as instructed and met a man coming up the lane and before I could say anything he said, "Get to hell out of here or I'll shoot you." I retreated in some amazement. I did not know what was going on. I met Christopher and told him the story and it transpired that he was a well-known IRA activist in the area. We went back to the farmer and told him the story and we could not help but being amused at his reply, "Oh, that would be agin the law!" We could only assume that he must have had some arms or explosives hidden where I was heading. The woodcock shooting at that time was very good and we had many great days shooting in the forestry around there. I remember one day shooting five woodcock out of a comparatively small wood.

My great enjoyment of shooting was always that of snipe and woodcock. This was however not to the exclusion of having the occasional day at driven pheasant and duck shoots. Driven pheasants shoots as sport can mean many things. To have very large bags it is necessary to have a top keeper and to breed a large number of birds. This works to the satisfaction of dedicated and experienced shots provided that the woods and terrain are suitable for giving the birds a sporting chance of evading the guns. Shooting birds on flat woodlands does not give the birds a chance to obtain enough elevation before they are fired at. I have said many times that a sportsman firing at low birds is very annoyed if he misses them but gets no satisfaction from bringing them down.

I strongly believe that many of the people participating in big, organized, driven shoots are obsessed by greed. Who wants a five-or-six hundred-bird day? I certainly never have or never would. In my youth we had a small pheasant shoot at Bellinter. My father reared two or three hundred birds. When they were fit to be released they were let off in the extensive woods and left to look after themselves, and not fed. We would shoot no more than twice a season and get around 75 to 80 birds each shoot. My goodness, how they flew. I seldom ever saw a low bird. Every one of them had to be shot high up in the beech trees. That was sport to me. Likewise we had a great population of mallard duck on the River Boyne behind the house. We never fed them but left them in peace and only shot them no more than three times in the season. That was sportsmanship without greed or material satisfaction.

The whole concept of these large pheasant shoots comes back to money. The larger the bags, the more money that can be charged to the aspiring guns. The quality and the taste of the hand fed birds are considerably inferior to that of the wild pheasant. If this is not so why do these large shoots find it almost impossible to get a market for a great number of their birds?

The greatest thrill to a youngster is to shoot his first driven woodcock. The second best thrill is to walk bogs all day after snipe. I virtually never shot without having a good Labrador retriever. It is anathema to me to shoot a bird and not to pick it up, particularly if it happens to be wounded. I witnessed quite a number of rather extraordinary and sometimes amusing incidents. On one occasion my bank manager, Ted Breslin and I, took a very good American friend out snipe shooting. He had never shot a snipe until he downed one in a very small bog. We only had Ted's dog out that day and it seemed unbelievable that he could not find the bird that had fallen just in front of us. We gave up, but I told Ted to keep a good look out as to what his dog passed the next day. I am still convinced that the dog must have swallowed him. On another occasion when shooting with a Russian friend, the same thing happened with one of my dogs!

I had a young dog out one day. I hit a snipe hard, which fluttered off over a hill quite a distance away. To my annoyance, the dog broke loose and took off and the last I saw of him was disappearing over the hill. About ten minutes later the dog appeared with my snipe. He must have chased the bird a long way, quite an achievement for a young dog.

Having made the observations about large driven pheasant shoots, I do wish to acknowledge that I had many very enjoyable days when invited to some of our local shoots by Bill Kruger, Johnnie Pollock, Lord Mount Charles, and others. They were all very well run and invariably the company was excellent and one met so many interesting people.

Louise became very much interested in training young Labradors and in bringing them to pheasant shoots to pick up. She was greatly encouraged by her great friend, Ruth Tennison who was generally regarded as the queen of the Labrador handlers in Ireland.

The pup, called *Rex*, that came from Hugo Kindersley turned out not only to be the best dog I had ever had but left five generations of superb dogs after him. At one time I thought that I had lost the breed when my incumbent dog died. Then I remembered that I had given the service of him to a girl who worked for a friend of ours and whose husband had a nice bitch, for he was a keen shooting man. I rang my friend to enquire where this man lived and she said, "Oh, did you not hear? He is in jail, convicted of having robbed a bank." This was unwelcome news; however, I found out where they lived and I went to see his wife. The man's bitch, that my last dog had serviced, had a lovely litter of pups so I acquired another excellent dog. I called him 'my rebel dog.'

Eventually I lost the breed. The last one I had of the breed, another very good dog, developed a hip disease that was considered hereditary, with the result that people with good bitches did not want to breed from him. I have had good dogs since but the Kindersley breed stood out. The pleasure that those dogs gave to both Louise and to me was very great indeed.

After shoots Louise would often say, "I picked up so many runners today." She was referring to wounded birds that had been caught running in the woods. I am convinced that a lot of the runners were not shot at all. As there were usually lots of pheasant in the woods and lots of young dogs about, I think that the dogs got at a lot of them.

It is sad that fishing now is nothing like it used to be either. Many factors have been responsible for this, mainly pollution and over-netting of the Atlantic salmon. I still keep a boat on Lough Owel and although I would be very hungry if relying on what I catch to keep me alive, it is such a joy to be out on this lovely unpolluted late. It is thought to be the cleanest lake in Ireland primarily because it is fed by springs; no river runs into it.

27.River and Lake Cruises

IN OCTOBER 1983 Louise and I first went cruising on the Shannon with Charlie and Sister Bird and two of their close friends from the United States, Bobbie and Ruthie Wolcott. We went down the river from Carrick-on-Shannon to Rooskey. It is such a peaceful and beautiful river and there are so many interesting places to stop off and see and explore. There are also plenty of excellent restaurants that are readily accessible from the river.

Coming back up the river we went north up to Lough Key and spent a night on the old King Harmon estate, Rockingham. Unfortunately the lovely old house, steeped in history, was burnt down some years ago. The estate has been taken over by the local county council that has made a most attractive park and has laid out many pleasant walks through the woods.

We moved from there up to Leitrim village. Unfortunately one of our heads (lavatories) got blocked up. Charlie went to the local pub and made enquires for the loan of a plunger to free it. Nobody seemed to know what a plunger was until suddenly a lad in the corner said "Oh, I know what you want, a sucker!" He got up from his seat, went off home and returned with the 'sucker' that did the job. We got really good weather and we learnt that it is much more pleasant to go in the autumn than in the busy time in mid summer. At that time one can hire a boat for considerably less and one avoids crowds on the river and lakes which make it quite difficult to find places to berth.

We took a trip starting from Portumna in 1988 and travelled up river to Athlone stopping off on the way at Clonmacnoise. This is a very ancient place on the banks of the river with interesting ruins. In the Dark Ages it was a famous seat of learning and scholarship. During its heyday the Vikings raided it on several occasions. That part of the river is not so interesting and goes through a lot of bog land so we came back down the river to Portumna to go down Lough Derg to Killaloe. Unfortunately when we returned to Portumna a hurricane blew up and we were unable to go out on the lake so that we had to cut our trip short.

In the eighteenth century a canal had been built to join up two of the great inland waterways of Ireland, the Shannon and the Erne. After some years of not paying its way it was abandoned. Charlie Haughey, who, in the early 1990s, was Taoiseach, decided that with co-operation from Northern Ireland, that the locks should be rebuilt and that the canal should be opened again.

In October 1995 Charlie, Sister, Louise and I along with a group of friends took a cruise up the reopened canal. The company was great and we had a lot of fun. Our first setback was when we were stuck in a lock for about two hours. A card system operates the new locks whereby one inserts a card in the controls and the lock gates open or shut, whichever one wants. Unfortunately the electricity went off when we were in a lock. The outgoing lock gates were just opening slightly when all stopped. It did not worry us of course but we wondered how long we would be trapped.

Continuing down the canal the next mishap occurred when we missed the turn into Keshcarrigan. We particularly wished to call there as we had been informed that there was a very good restaurant and pub in the village. In turning around we first hit the dingy against the bank and knocked the outboard motor off which very luckily fell on the bank. Having retrieved that, we proceeded back on our course and then came upon a cruiser that had run aground on the side of the canal. People on board threw us a rope and we tried to pull them off and went aground ourselves. A tractor arrived then and threw a rope, which we grabbed and got pulled off going down stream again. We did not try anymore to get to

Keshcarrigan and left the other boat aground! I presume they got off later.

We continued up to Ballyconnell where the younger group, which included my daughter, Lorraine, her husband, John, and a friend of theirs, Alan Cox, went up the town to have a few drinks and to look around. The Birds, Joanie Moore, widow of the horse trainer Dan Moore, and myself, went to have a look at the Ballyconnell hotel. We returned to our boat and decided we would retire to bed. Joanie, who was leaving in the morning, came out of her cabin and said, "My handbag containing car keys and money is missing". I went to search around but no sign. Charlie and Sister had gone to bed and I said "Better have a look around their cabin". "No, don't do that", said Joanie, "It could not have got in there". Shortly afterwards a police car arrived on the jetty and an officer enquired "Everything alright?" "Well, actually, no". said Joanie, "My handbag has disappeared." "We will have to see about that at once", said the police officers and drove off quickly. They went into all the pubs in Ballyconnell and cleared them looking for a likely thief. All the locals were quite amazed and had never witnessed the pubs being summarily closed before.

John, Lorraine and Alan arrived back to the boat and complained that they had been thrown out of the pub because someone had lost her handbag. When they learned of what had happened Lorraine said "Oh, I put that in Charlie and Sister's cabin as I thought it would be safer there." Joanie became known as the first woman who had ever had all the pubs in Ballyconnell closed up before the time that the licensing laws ordain.

Continuing, we reached Belturbet, a pleasant town, where we changed some of our crew. That evening we decided to have our dinner at Butler's Bridge not far away. Piling into one car we did not have enough room for all and Colin Magnier said, "Put me in the boot." That was all right except that coming into Butler's Bridge Jessica Magnier put her indicator out to go left and we turned right. The next moment there was a squad car after us and wanted to know what we were up to putting our indicator out the wrong way. That was all right, but they might have been more aggressive if they had known there was a body in the boot!

Our trip down Upper Lough Erne was pleasant but uneventful. We berthed under Portora in Enniskillen. I, being an old Portoran, Charlie said we must go up and see my old school. He rang the headmaster who was most amenable and said "Come up in the morning and I'll show you around." My daughter had damaged her ankle and Charlie said "I shall order a taxi to bring us up to the school." The taxi arrived and he said "one two many, I can only take five." Colin said "Don't worry, I'll walk." We set off and the traffic was so dense in Enniskillen that Colin was sitting on a bench on Portora before we arrived! We returned to Belturbet and so ended that trip.

Our next trip was in 1996 when we again we went up the Shannon-Erne Canal. Our crew this time was my sister, Stella Smith, my cousin, Jean Ellis with her husband, Herbie, and my cousin, Charles Leatham, from Zimbabwe. We went up the canal to Enniskillen and then returned to Carrick-on-Shannon. The only excitement we had on that trip was when we were coming down the canal. I was up top and Charles was steering the boat. Suddenly, for no apparent reason, the boat went straight for the bank. I luckily grabbed the wheel and no doubt avoided a big disaster since Charles was apt always to drive the boat at full throttle. He had fallen asleep!

In June 1998 we had the same crew except that Charles wasn't with us. We set out from Portumna and fairly quickly made Athlone. Returning down the river near Shannonbridge, we decided to go up the River Suck. We knew that work was going on there to give access to

Ballinasloe but no way was it on the charts. Much to the consternation of our females we went up and arrived suddenly at a dead end. Turning with difficulty, and as it was getting dark; we did not know where to berth. Necessity is the mother of invention and we managed to manoeuvre to a bush, to which we tied up for the night. No doubt but we were lucky not to have been shipwrecked; however, we survived and went right down to Killaloe on Lough Derg. The rest was uneventful; however, it did become clear to us that the busy season is not enjoyable and we decided that, in the future, it would have to be September. On that trip we were continually out of water, which we could not understand. It entailed berthing to frequently replenish our water tank, a task that was extremely difficult in the busy season because of the demand for water at the various jetties and quays. On returning to Portumna it was discovered that our water was leaking into the bilge.

During September 1999, with the same crew again we took off down the river from Carrick-on-Shannon. Our first excitement came at Roosky. There is a bridge there, which has to be lifted for the larger cruisers. We had not read our manual carefully enough and came cruising down oblivious to this fact. As we approached it down stream we suddenly realized that we might not fit. We could not stop in time and being on the top deck threw ourselves flat. The steering wheel cleared with about 3 inches to spare! We heard afterwards that several boats had been badly damaged there. On leaving Lough Forbes we went down the Camlin River, which is connected to the Shannon beside Termonbarry by means of a canal. Down the canal we went and found a very dilapidated lock with nobody around. We came to the conclusion that it must be closed and there being no room to turn the boat the only solution seemed to go back up the canal in reverse! It is only about half a mile long but there was great difficulty in getting the large cruiser back up, bouncing off bushes and trees. We berthed at the top of the canal and walked to Richmond Harbour at Clondara and discovered that the lock was in use and the lock keeper lived there. So we went back down the canal and eventually got back onto the River Shannon.

We then went down the river to Lanesborough and into Lough Ree. This is a dangerous lake with a lot of rocks and we were well aware of this. We decided to go to Portrunny on the west shore and were, we thought, following the markings carefully when suddenly there was a bang and we were up on a shoal of rocks! Panic stations! The girls started waving flags and putting life jackets on themselves and us. Herbie Ellis, who had been a very famous doctor pilot in the Fleet Air Arm, kept saying, "I should be court-martialled for this!" I could not help being somewhat amused with all the antics. I quietly said to Herbie "Put her in reverse and we may come off." The girls would not have this, as they feared we might sink. As there was a considerable shoal of rocks I considered even if we did we would be above water. We called for assistance by means of our mobile telephone and in quite a short time a crew from the Emerald Star Line appeared in one of their boats, which they had commandeered, and pulled us off and very fortunately there was no damage done.

We went upstream past Carrick-on-Shannon into Lough Key. There were two cruisers going up into Lough Key out of the Boyle River. We were cruising up the lake to go to Boyle and on looking across I saw that the two boats had stopped and shortly afterwards I noticed a girl swimming from one boat to the others with a rope. "My God," I said, "They are aground!" We turned back and went into the harbour at Rockingham and I said, "What is the betting that the crew from Emerald Star Line will be waiting to commandeer our boat?" Sure enough there they were and out we had to go to rescue them. It was quite a coincidence that we had to be rescued and then had to go to the rescue. The two boats were crewed by Germans who plied us with schnapps on our return to Rockingham. This ended a very enjoyable and quite eventful trip.

The same crew again took off from Belturbet to go down the River Erne in September 2000. We stopped off at Crom Castle in Co. Fermanagh and saw some interesting things there. Crom Castle is in the care of the UK National Trust. The new castle is the home of Lord Erne. The ruins of the old castle alongside the lake are quite impressive and the yew trees there are the oldest and largest in these islands. It is like being inside a house when under them. We pushed onto Enniskillen where we spent a night berthed under Portora and then on to Beleek on the west end of Lower Lough Erne the next day. Beleek is a most interesting old town straddling the border and is world famous for its porcelain. Coming back up the lake on the north shore we visited a rather unique island called Lusty Beg, which adjoins Boa Island from which there is a chain ferry bringing cars and lorries to a summer resort on Lusty Beg. I understand Fermanagh County Council, which puts on functions and concerts there, runs it. Moving on we spent the night in Castle Archdale. This is a splendidly wooded old estate that is also funded by the county council. The remainder of the trip was most enjoyable and relaxing and we got back to Belturbet and packed up for home.

1n 2001 we had the same crew again. We set out from Portumna and went down to Mountshannon in the most glorious weather. We sat out on the upper deck and had our lunch' there lying in the sunshine. We moved down the lake to Scarrif, which is tucked away in a lovely little harbour. We decided then not to go any further south and went across the lake to Dromineer and from there up the east side. On Tuesday, 11th September, we sailed up the lake and pulled into Terryglass. An elderly man was on the pier and he was crying and kept saying, "It's terrible, it's terrible." We had not had our wireless turned on and that was the first we had heard of the disaster at the Twin Towers, New York. Of course this blighted the remainder of our trip back up to Shannonbridge and Ballinasloe. Herbie was very heavily involved in Lloyds and indeed later lost a great deal of money in the disaster but to his great credit he continued on our trip without complaint but thinking of all the poor people who had been killed and disabled in the atrocity. We returned to Portumna amid great sadness.

Little did I know that within a week I would face the saddest day of my life when my dear Louise to whom I had been very happily married for fifty four years died suddenly.

We move on again to September 2002. We had the same crew again except that Jean Wilson, who was to become my wife, joined us. Starting from Carrick-on-Shannon we went down river into Lough Ree. We certainly kept our eyes open for rocks this time! We called at Lecarrow on the west side. Lecarrow is a most attractive village that is connected to the lake by a canal which was built to ferry stone down to Athlone for building there a hundred and fifty years or more, ago. We stayed a night in Athlone and then moved up the west side to Glasson where we dined in an excellent restaurant on the lakeshore. We proceeded up river through Lanesborough, back to Carrick-on-Shannon, onto Lough Key and to Boyle, where a new marina has been constructed. The weather was beautiful and we ate and drank on the upper deck in brilliant sunshine. There was heavy fog on the final morning and we had quite a job to get back to base at Carrick but we made it and another lovely trip had ended.

On our last trip in September 2003, we returned to Belturbet and did the Erne trip again. We saw many of the interesting places, which we had seen previously in 2000. One very interesting place that we visited on this trip was Tully Castle on the south side of Lower Lough Erne. It is a mediaeval castle set upon a high hill overlooking the lake; it was the seat of one of the old Irish chiefs with an interesting history from distant times. It has an attractive seventeenth century garden on the east side of the castle and also a centre where one can read about the history of the place. On our return to Belturbet we stopped off at a pier near Galloon to have our lunch'. Jean and I discovered a most unusual little graveyard nearby tucked away between trees. On looking at some of the gravestones we noticed that many of them had a skull and crossbones on the top. Although we made some enquiries in Beltubet, nobody knew what they were meant to represent. So ended this last visit to the Shannon-Erne waterway. I consider myself so lucky to have been on so many trips on this magnificent waterway and of course with such happy and convivial company.

28. Religion

RELIGION, which is sometimes a rather controversial subject in Ireland, is something that I believe should be supported regardless of denominational allegiance. I belong to the Protestant Church of Ireland community, and say that I have never experienced any bigotry or unfriendliness from any member of any other religious persuasion. Indeed, many of my best friends are of a different religion. We are predominately all Christians and should behave as such. I was educated at Portora, Enniskillen and in my time saw very little bigotry or hatred there. Unfortunately that does not seem to be the case in Northern Ireland and all decent people despair that some people there cannot live peacefully together. "Not an inch" continues to be the cry from both sides and we can only hope and pray that sometime strong leaders will see sense and stop the hatred in our lovely country.

My great grandfather, Francis, was rector of Kilmessan parish for 40 years. It is in the cemetery there that he and his family down to my father and mother are buried. Like many other small churches it was closed around the 1960s, which was a pity but I suppose it was inevitable owing to the lack of parishioners. I understand that my father and mother changed their allegiance from Kilmessan to Bective when they took over Bellinter. I am not sure of the exact reason but I believe that my father did not much like the rector in Kilmessan and much approved of the Bective incumbent.

All my life I attended and loved Bective church. It was a little gem in beautiful surroundings. When I married Louise she took over as treasurer and did a wonderful job in restoring the finances as well as the church and the cemetery around it. It was a tremendous disappointment to me that when Bishop Empey became Bishop of Meath and Kildare in the early 1990s, that the first thing he stated was that he proposed to shut 33 churches in his diocese. In spite of my fighting all the way he persisted in shutting our lovely little church. This was a most regressive step as we were very viable, and had just recently done up the church which was in excellent condition and the large graveyard was very well kept. Our bishop refused to listen. Bolton, who had built the church in 1853, was interred with his wife and nephew in the vault under the church. The church was sold and therefore it had to be deconsecrated and the bodies had to be removed and re-interred. The removal was not at all pleasant, as the coffins had collapsed with obvious results. At the re-internment in the graveyard I remarked to the bishop "I'm sure Bolton, who built this lovely church would not feel very happy with you."

The parish church at Trim, that is the cathedral, was to be responsible for the upkeep of the cemetery. It was totally neglected and rapidly went wild and overgrown. I personally took over and to a large extent, after very much hard work, got it back into reasonable shape. We were lucky to get *Fás* representatives to come in and cut the grass around the graves. I told the bishop very plainly that a large number of those 33 churches he proposed to close would close anyway as they had no support left. "Why," I asked, "do you insist on closing one that is viable?" All my protestations fell on deaf ears and so ended the life of our lovely little church

Bective church was viable. The Bird family had made a bequest to the church, the benefit of which has now passed to Trim Cathedral. Shortly before the church was closed we had done it up and we had enough money to continue. Our congregation was of from twelve to fourteen, sometimes more, sometimes less. I tried to influence the bishop's decision regarding closure, but to no avail. It is now a home to John Ryan, the well-known painter, who has opened an art gallery there.

Our rector for many years at Bective was the late Dean Breedon of Trim. When he passed away, Alan Barrett, who

had previously been rector at Navan, became the dean.
Andrew Furlong succeeded Alan Barrett sometime in the
1990s and became the Dean of Clonmacnoise. Andrew
Furlong is a nice man, was a very good pastor and everyone
liked him. He was ecumenical in outlook and got on
very well with the parish priest. However, in late 2001 he
declared that Jesus was not divine. In 2002 he was tried for
heresy and later on he was dismissed. The man's position was
untenable.

My family donated the sites for both graveyards at
Kilmessan village to both the Catholic and Protestant
churches. One of our neighbours was Mattie Quinn of Asigh.
He lived in a stone-built cottage up in the fields. He had four
or five sons. Mattie was a very nice old man in the nineteen
forties. It was quite a walk from Mattie's cottage up to
Bellinter House. One day old Mattie came up, he was huffing
and puffing, as he was a big, heavy man. He met my father
and told him that he was very concerned about getting a
burial plot in the Catholic graveyard at Kilmessan. He said
that he had been to see the then parish priest but the priest
refused to give him a plot. Poor Mattie was very upset. My
father said to him, "Now, Mattie, you don't worry yourself.
I'll pick you up in two days' time and we'll see about it."

As arranged, my father picked up Mattie and drove to
Kilmessan to see the parish priest who wasn't a very nice
man. My father discussed Mattie's concern with the priest
and said to him, 'You know, my family presented all this land
for the graveyard. Mattie is going to have a plot here and I
am going to choose it." My father went out and chose a very
good plot, right beside the church for Mattie. The priest said,
"Oh, oh, this is terrible, this is terrible. That's my valuable,
valuable plot." "Well", said my father, "That is where Mattie
is going." That was that. My father was very annoyed with
the priest having dear old Mattie all worried over a plot.

Some of my closest friends were Catholic priests. When I
was quite young I remember meeting a wonderful priest

called Father Poland, who was administrator in Navan for many years and finished up parish priest of Rathkenny. I only knew him when I was very young, but what a lovely man he was.

He used to hunt with the Tara Harriers when my father was master and huntsman. My father told me many stories about him but one certainly stuck in my memory. A certain man called Boyle had done a considerable amount of work on the kennels for my father and had been well paid for doing so. He owned a farm off the Commons Road, near Navan. One day the Tara harriers were hunting there. The hounds ran on to Boyle's farm and he came out and berated my father for doing so. Father Poland was out hunting that day and rode up to Boyle and said "Disgraceful, you will suffer for this".

A short time later my father had some cattle for sale one morning early on the Fair Green at Navan. He was sitting outside the rails of the parochial house when suddenly there was quite a commotion down further on the green. Someone ran up to the parochial house and shortly afterwards Father Poland appeared and rushed down to the green. Returning after a little while he spotted my father sitting near the rails and came over to him and said "Cecil, do you know what that was?" "I have no idea," said my father. "It was Boyle who has had a stroke, now do you believe in my religion?" he jokingly enquired.

On another occasion when my father was also selling cattle on the Fair Green early on an extremely cold morning, Father Poland came out and saw my father sitting by the rails and walked over and gave him a poke through the rails and said "You look very cold, come on in for a while," which he did. The priest's housekeeper appeared and he said to her "Bring up some convent cow's milk", whereupon a bottle of champagne and canapés appeared. "Ah," said Father Poland, "None of your Protestant cows can give milk like this."

One of the finest men I have met in my life was Dr. O'Dwyer. He was head of the Maynooth Mission to China who, having come up from Dangans, Co. Mayo, had purchased a neighbouring estate, Dowdstown, for the congregation. They built a magnificent building that they named *Dalgan Park*, where priests were trained to go to the Far East and other deprived areas of the world. Dr. O'Dwyer was a very personal friend to all our family and indeed when the Eucharistic Congress was held in Ireland in 1932 my father offered Bellinter to accommodate clergy and priests for the occasion. When in my teens I was suffering from quite severe bronchitis Dr. O'Dwyer said prayers for me.

He was a great sportsman and a famous hurler in his younger days. He also played golf. He also was a very keen fisherman and caught many salmon on the Boyne. He was just as interested in shooting although I must add that his ability to put anything in the bag was very limited. We used to have a very enjoyable shoot in Bellinter when my father reared a few hundred pheasants. We did not get big bags but the quality of the shooting was magnificent. The birds flew very high and very strong. The doctor decided that we should amalgamate the shoots between Dowdstown and Bellinter as he had very good woods there. The shoots would start in Dowdstown at about 11.30 in the morning and after about an hour or so we would have a break and were royally entertained by the doctor. After this sojourn the quality of the shooting deteriorated radically until we adjourned for lunch' at Bellinter at about 2pm. I remember at one time in the afternoon that Aubrey Brabazon had shot a rabbit and next thing the doctor said, "I'm shot!" This was quite extraordinary, as he had fired in the other direction. Undoubtedly it was a ricochet, which proved the point that shots should not be fired at ground game in an organized shoot. While on that subject, I remember my father standing between Dr. O'Dwyer and Dr. Dunne when a rabbit ran out and both fired from each side of him. He was very crippled but said, "I never realized I could jump", but did so.

The doctor had an old hammer gun and going across country, shooting with him was quite a hazardous adventure. On reaching a fence he would hand me his gun fully loaded pointed at me and say, "Hold this while I get over". However, I survived. I used to go fishing with him also and we had many fishing trips together. Dr. Dunne another administrator in Navan for many years, was a very keen follower of the Tara Harriers and in fact became chairman of the hunt. I used sometimes meet him in Navan on a morning that we would be hunting, dressed up in all his clerical clothes but with his hunting boots under his surplice. "I have a funeral to conduct but I'll give a quick service so don't move off too soon," he would say.

In the old days when the clergy had to ride horses to do their duties they had what was called the oats and hay collection. The doctor, having two or three hunters, decided he would revive the oats collection, much to the annoyance of some of his parishioners. I met a good friend, Tom Marsh, one day in Navan and he said, "Have you heard that the doctor is riding his horse backwards through Navan?" "What are you talking about?" I said, "Yes, he wants to see what quality of oats he's getting!"

He was a very good chairman of our hunt and also a shooting man. The bishop got a bit upset with all his sporting activities and decided to banish him to a parish at the farthest end of his diocese, Tubber, near Moate. This did not deter the doctor in the least and within one year he was chairman of the Westmeath hunt!

I used to go sometimes, on his invitation, to hunt one of his horses in Westmeath. On one occasion, my wife Louise, Neenie Cameron and I went down to have dinner at the parochial house and to stay the night. Having been wined and dined very well Louise and Neenie went to bed. The doctor and I had a couple more drinks and I said "I am off to bed, where is my room?" "Oh up the stairs and on the right was the reply". Not wishing to awaken my wife I undressed outside the door and slipped into bed. I soon discovered that I was in bed with a blonde and my wife was a brunette. That took a bit of explaining next morning. However, Dr. Dunne was a good pastor and priest and we had some very happy times together.

More recently, I have known Fr. Declan Smith for quite a long time. He is another very sporting man and has hunted a bit with the harriers and the Meath Foxhounds. He was curate in Trim and Courtown for some years and is now parish priest beside Lough Derravarragh. He is a very good shot and always has had first class dogs. During the season his score of shooting cock pheasant is very impressive. He has for several years brought out some of his friends, including me, to shoot snipe and woodcock up in the Cavan country. Those outings have always been most enjoyable.

I have met more very good and sporting priests in my hunting time; I would mention Father Kearney and Father Conlon, all of whom have been a great asset to our hunting in Co Meath.

29. Marriage to Jean, Trip to the U.S.A.

O NE YEAR after Louise had passed away, Jean and I announced that we were to be married. There were lots of things to do in dealing with the clergy and such. Mr. Clarke, who was the rector at Navan, was particularly helpful.

Some time before our wedding and before arrangements had been considered in any great detail, Charlie Bird and I went down to see Avia in Co. Kildare. Avia brought us out to lunch' to Rathsallagh Hotel, near Dunlavin. It is a lovely spot. Joe Flynn and his wife, Kay, the owners of the place, have done a tremendous job of work down there. They have a hotel and a golf course. I got talking to Joe whom I had never met before. It turned out that Joe is from Cork. We spent about an hour talking about Cork and it transpired that he knew all the people whom I knew in Cork when I used to go hunting down there a long time ago. We had a very pleasant day and that's when I first saw Rathsallagh.

Afterwards Jean and I were thinking about where to have the wedding reception. Jean's brother, Alan lives very close to Rathsallagh, near Dunlavin. Talking about this, Jean said to me, "Wouldn't Rathsallagh be a grand place to have the reception?" I agreed. Jean thought for a while and said that it was too far away if we were going to get married in Co. Meath. I said to her, "What about Dunlavin? What about seeing the clergyman there who is Alan's rector?" So that started the whole thing.

Later in a conversation with Alan when I was making enquiries about the possibility of getting married in Dunlavin, Alan said, "Oh, we have a new rector down here now and is name is Declan Smith." I had to laugh because I thought that my old pal, Father Declan Smith had changed sides. However, he is not the same man. Fr. Smith is still at Crookedwood. Later when people asked me who was marrying us, I'd say, "Declan Smith." Well, they all stopped and looked at me.

Alan arranged that we meet Rev. Declan Smith in Dunlavin. He agreed to marry us. Dunlavin is in the Dublin archdiocese so that we had to go to Rathmines in Dublin, to the Church of Ireland offices to give details and to get permission to marry. Afterwards we went back down to Dunlavin and met Rev. Declan Smith again. He brought us to the church and showed us around. He is a great man to sing. He began to sing hymns that we might choose to have sung on our wedding day. We went with his advice.

Avia arranged to have a party for me on the night before the wedding and also arranged that Charlie, Sister and myself would stay the night with Willie Robinson, who lives nearby, and whom I have known for a long time.

Charlie and Sister arrived at Craystown from the U.S. but Charlie was in a bit of a state as he was over the age at which he could hire a car in this country and had to travel down by taxi from Dublin Airport. He was a bit angry because of that. I told him not to worry as that I'd get permission from my insurance company to permit him to drive one of my cars. So that was all right. The plan was that I would drive down to Willie Robinson's on the day before the wedding. Charlie and Sister were to drive down to have lunch' with Avia.

The next thing was that we had terrible rain and terrible floods. That was 15th November 2002. The countryside was flooded. Anyway, Charlie took off with Sister in my little car. I was worried about them. I could see them floating off into a field or worse. When I was in contact with them on that evening, Charlie told me that the little car was great and that it got through the lot very well.

When I was coming into Kilcock from the Summerhill side the little river there had burst its banks so that there were three feet of water in the dip in the road there. The car I was driving was stuck between two lorries, one in front of me and one behind me and with two lorries coming towards me sending big waves of water up to the top of my car door. I didn't know if I was going to get through it or not. Somehow I got through and on the way met other bad floods but not so bad as that one at Kilcock Eventually I arrived down at Willie's and told him that I was lucky to have been there at all with the roads the way they were.

Robert Hall and his wife were to come to the party and were to collect Peter Curling and bring him also. This was to be a surprise for me. Robert was driving from Tattersalls at Fairyhouse to his home in Co. Kildare when he ran into severe flooding at Batterstown. The Tolka River had burst its banks with the effect that the water rose rapidly on the road and swamped his car. A lorry stopped in the floods and the driver beckoned to Robert to try to make it to the lorry. Robert had his terrier with him in the car. He rescued his dog and waded through the flood to the lorry where the lorry driver gave him a pull up into the cab. He had to abandon his car. The lorry driver took him to Batterstown village where his wife came and collected him. However, they and Peter Curling didn't make it to the party. Down at Willie's we heard that poor Robert was nearly drowned.

That evening at Willie's the gang at the dinner party were all saying to me, "Ah, sure, there won't be any wedding tomorrow." You see, Jean wasn't coming down until the following morning from Boltown with her sister, Ruth. "Ah, you might as well get drunk," they said; "Jean will be floating away in the floods." I was getting horrid worried then. By God, I was getting worried. Afterwards I learned that Jean had telephoned Charlie Angel who lives near Kilcock and that Charlie had told her not to come near Kilcock as the floods were bad and that she would be washed away. "Keep away from here, wherever you go," he said. So Jean and Ruth went off around Edenderry or somewhere miles away on a big detour to make sure that they would escape the floods. They arrived safely, which was a great relief to me.

Jean went first to her brother's place to change and I eventually went to the church. I was waiting there with Alan and chatting. We were waiting and waiting and there was no sign of Jean. "By God," said I, "Have there been more floods?" She appeared all right and things got underway. I don't think that I had a best man. There were witnesses there, and of course, John and Lorraine were there and also Jean's two daughters, Sheelin and Susan.

After the wedding we went to Rathsallagh and we had a wonderful party there. The owner, Joe, was great gas and his wife was charming. They put on a great show for us. We were all very impressed and very pleased. It was great. Joe and his wife were invited too and Joe made out a poem about Jean and myself. Joe has that talent that he can write about anything on the spot. Alan, Jean's brother, was very good also as he has a similar talent. We had a great day!

Charlie and Sister were, like Jean and myself, staying at the Rathsallagh Hotel and during their stay, Charlie got up to have a bath or a shower, I have forgotten which, and there was no water. Charlie got in touch with the management and said, "There's no bloody water here." The pump had gone wrong. Nothing happened anyway so between the hopping and the jumping, Charlie got dressed and went out with Sister. Unaware to Charlie at the time, he had left the plug in the bath and the tap open. On their return to their room they found it flooded. So, at the time of our wedding there were lots of floods. Things were floating around, outside and inside!

We didn't really have a honeymoon as such. Our wedding took place in the middle of the hunting and shooting seasons and, apart from that, Jean had things to do at Boltown and I had things to do at Craystown. However in the following spring, May 2003, we went to the United States to stay with Charlie and Sister. We had a wonderful time.

We boarded the 'plane for Boston on 29th May at Dublin Airport. We stopped off at Shannon Airport where we took a walk around the duty-free area. While looking around to buy a few presents, my name was called over the intercom. We rushed back to the information centre where I was told that I had been upgraded to first class from tourist class. "That's fine," I said, "But how about my wife?" I wasn't believed at first because Jean was travelling in her former name, Jean Wilson, as her passport showed. After some confusion we were told to wait. A little time passed when a young woman came to us and said that everything is fine and that we both were to be upgraded. A neighbour of ours at Craystown had just retired from Aer Lingus after 32 years of service. When she knew of our flight plan she told a friend of hers, a hostess on our flight, to try to upgrade me at Shannon airport. Our neighbour had forgotten to tell her former colleague that I was newly married and that I would be travelling with my wife. When we were in our first class seats the hostess could not have been kinder to us and we had the best of food.

Having arrived at Proctor Street, Manchester, Connecticut, we started on a round of lunch' and dinner parties where we met many old friends that Louise and I had known from previous visits. Living in luxury in Charlie and Sister's lovely home, we had a lovely time. We walked along the beautiful Singing Beach, through paths, and on roads where we passed some fabulous summer homes of very rich people. We visited the Myopia hunt kennels where we were given a show of the hounds and had a good look around, all arranged by Sister's brother, Bunny Sears, a most delightful man, who could not have been kinder to us. He and his wife, Barbara, gave a dinner party in our honour that was attended by hunt masters and other hunt members.

It is a lovely spot, Manchester, a beautiful spot right on the sea. We had a lovely week with Charlie and Sister and then the Sullivans, who had owned Boyne Hill, asked us to visit them. Pauline Sullivan said, "Oh, you must come down to New York to see us." Johnny, Pauline's son, whom I had known when he was a boy, has a beautiful place at Greenwich. He had been married but his marriage broke up. At present he has a girlfriend called Nonie. He had been over to Ireland on a visit with Nonie before Louise died. Nonie is a very nice person and Johnny couldn't have been nicer. Anyway, Johnny said, "You must come down and stay at my mother's place in New York." That was all arranged so we began to look up railway timetables and flights to see how we would get down to New York from Boston. Johnny rang up when we were at Charlie's and said, "Don't worry about that, I'll send a car to pick you up." Well, this big car arrived at Charlie's with a chauffeur and drove us right the way down to Greenwich. We had a wonderful trip down.

Johnny laid on a car for us the next day to take us to New York where Pauline had us put up in her club there for three nights. At lunchtime we met Pauline's youngest daughter, Chrissie, in the club and had a great chat about old times in Boyne Hill and Ireland. In the evening the two older girls, Pam Bamber and Leslie Horn, and their husbands, gave us a lovely dinner party in the River Club, which is right along the river in New York. We had a wonderful time there and then they said, "You must sing a song." I said, "This is a club, I can't do that." "Go on, go on," they said. I sang *Galway Bay* and there were tears coming down their faces.

The following day Johnnie showed us around his business where they produce many types of silk garments. We found that most interesting.

That evening we met Jean's daughter, Sheelin, who has a business in New York whereby she restores furniture and does gilding and the like. We saw her very comfortable flat and went out to dinner with her that night.

On the following day we went for a walk around Central Park that we found very interesting and impressive. That evening we said goodbye and boarded the plane at Kennedy Airport for Dublin. On our return journey, the same hostess was on duty again but was not able to up-grade us, as there were no vacant seats in the first class section. However, she knew that we were on our honeymoon and gave us a couple of drinks that were greatly appreciated.

30. The Final Chapter

BEING a fairly active person, I was somewhat at a loose end when I was unable to continue riding after I had fallen from a young horse and had broken my neck. Although my neck has very limited movement, matters could have been worse.

Loving country life, I have always cultivated my garden. I find that it is satisfying and interesting to be able to provide fresh produce. The flavour of my home produce is so much better than that of which one may purchase in a supermarket.

My late wife, Louise, was a good grower of flowers as is my present, dear wife, Jean, so that we make a good combination.

With the arrival of the deep freezer a big change was made to our lives in so far that the amount of vegetables one could grow and thereby, freeze, increased. Such species as peas and various beans can be easily stored. I usually aim to grow enough to see us through the year. I am no expert and I have my failures but I enjoy the challenge. Work helps to keep me reasonably mobile. Also, I try to grow enough potatoes to do us until the next crop but I am not always successful in this. I do not use any artificial fertiliser but rather, farmyard manure.

I have a couple of small rotavators without such it would not be possible for me to accomplish what I take on to do. Weeds are always a great problem but I manage to keep them under control without using herbicides.

Many years ago while staying with the late Jim and Jill McAleese in their holiday home near Roundstone in Connemara, we had a lovely potato with our supper. I enquired as to what variety of potato it was and was told that it was a *Scarlet Pimpernel*. I had not heard of that variety before but was told that a local farmer grew a field of them each year. Jim gave me about a dozen small potatoes of the variety on my departure; when I returned home I planted them. They provided a good crop and proved to be lovely eaters. A few years later Jim telephoned me and told me that the farmer down at Roundstone had lost the breed and could not find the variety anywhere and was anxious to know if I had any. I sent him a small bag of seed potatoes and so kept the breed going from a few small spuds that I had brought up to Meath.

Although I am now over 84 years of age, my ambition is to stay above ground for as long as possible in order to enjoy many more years with my wife, family and with my good friends, of which I have many. Hunting, shooting, fishing, horse racing and Rugby are my main sporting interests. I still shoot and fish whenever I can. I also love parties and knocking out a good time and why not?

When I look back upon my life, I consider that fate has been kind to me. Even though I have been on this planet for a long time and can clearly recall events of the distant past when this State was in its very young years, my perception is that my life has passed quickly. As one ages, one's perception of time is that the clock speeds up. For a child, time seems to linger, later, as one gets older, it walks, then trots and then gallops like hell. With all the good days there have been sad and bad times too.

Health-wise I have always considered myself lucky. I contracted bronchitis quite badly in my teens and have had trouble with my sinuses all my life since. When I arise in the morning I find myself quite stuffed up nasally but as the day goes on the condition improves. Such a condition is merely a minor irritation in comparison to the suffering of those poor people who suffer from incurable illnesses. Indeed, I had to spend so much of my life watching dear Louise enduring incessant pain from acute arthritis. How I felt for her and considered myself so inadequate as nothing could have been done to relieve her distress. Louise was a lesson. She always used to put her best foot forward to the extent that not even her best friends were aware of the severity of her suffering.

I have had a good life from a health standpoint apart from sporting scares and a few near-hit accidents when farming. I attribute my good health to living an active life. Apart from sporting activity, I till and sow my vegetable garden and I mow my own lawns. I also go for walks to limber up the old bones. I eat lots of fresh vegetables and recently, I have begun to take a multivitamin tablet, a cod liver oil capsule and a vitamin E pill once a day.

Vitamin E is interesting. A little while ago an old veterinary friend, Ham Lambert, was interviewed on the Saturday morning farm programme. He is in his nineties. When asked to what he attributed his good health and long life, he replied, "I don't really know but I have been taking a 4 unit tablet of vitamin E daily for most of my life." I said to myself when I heard that that I had better try that stuff myself.

The following week I called into my local pharmacist and asked for 4 unit vitamin E pills. "That is extraordinary," he said. "I've sold very little of this for years but in the last few days there has been such a demand for it that it is sold out!" I explained the reason for this and we had a good laugh. The radio programme had been so well received that the station decided to repeat it within a few weeks of the original broadcast. My pharmacist had another big sale of vitamin E!

Over the years I have seen many changes in Irish life. Up to 1962 we did not have a television station in Ireland, now we have two stations and a total of four channels. There were very few cars on the roads when I was young and indeed not so many around until the nineteen eighties, I suppose. Nearly every adult and adolescent has a motorcar nowadays. Everybody has a mobile telephone, from children to adults. I can't remember if we had a telephone when we lived at Bellinter. Everyone appears to have money whereas before few had it. That is progress and it is a good thing.

Even though Ireland is supposed to be the fourth richest country in the world, a standing that is obviously arrived at by using questionable criteria, one would not think that we are in that league when one addresses the condition of our country roads and the state of the street surfaces in towns such as Navan and Trim. There is a strong Third World look about them. A friend of mine said to me that the last time he had seen a street surface as bad as that of Railway Street in Navan was in Kumasi in Ghana in the late 1980s. It is hard to understand how this is so. County councils probably do not use their income wisely. Waste is killing this country. Waste of resources, that is. Soon a bunch of county councilors from Meath will head off to Peru or Chile or some other such country for a few weeks at the public's expense to inspect volcanoes there and to see the damage caused by past eruptions just in case a volcano might erupt in Co. Meath. One never hears of local politicians from other countries coming over here to inspect our roads in order to see what happens when the policy of neglect is rigidly enforced.

For five or six years, maybe more, there has been a lot of discussion about possible routes of the proposed M3 motorway that is to connect the Clonee bypass northwestwards to the border with Northern Ireland. So far as I know the route of the proposed motorway has been decided upon, which means that the motorway will run to the northeast of the present road, the N3, in that immediate area between the hills of Skryne and Tara, and to continue northwestwards.

Tara is undoubtedly one of the most important archeological sites in Ireland and I consider it completely inappropriate to run a motorway through the proposed route. Many times I have stood on the hill looking at the most wonderful views of the countryside. The whole mystical and historical importance of this wonderful spot will be shattered by the constant sight and noise of traffic destroying the peace and tranquility. Of course I recognize the necessity of having a greatly improved road system for the commuters to Dublin and would be prepared to accept the proposed one by Tara if there were no alternative.

There are, of course, other possible routes, which in my opinion are much more viable. A motorway, which is to run through Ashbourne and onwards to Slane, is under construction at present. Why not build a branch off that to the north of Navan and to run on to Kells? The National Roads Authority (NRA) just say that is not viable but give no reason why.

The most important requirement is a railway connection. The existing railway from Navan to Drogheda goes under the Dublin-Slane motorway. Why not construct a branch from that along the motorway to the city? It appears that our great planners in the N.R.A. have very little foresight. The NRA does not permit the building of services just off the motorways meaning that drivers have to leave those roads and go into towns to purchase fuel and food. This defeats one of the purposes of motorways, which is to by-pass towns. That's the civil service and political party hacks for you!

There are, of course, vested interests involved in developing housing estates along the motorway. The prospect of a building development and an interchange junction alongside Tara is completely unacceptable in my view.

I am leaving my pen down now and I look forward to the years to come with my dear wife, Jean, my family and friends. And, I'll keep singing.